Caro aluno, seja bem-vindo à sua plataforma do conhecimento!

A partir de agora, está à sua disposição uma plataforma que reúne, em um só lugar, recursos educacionais digitais que complementam os livros impressos e foram desenvolvidos especialmente para auxiliar você em seus estudos. Veja como é fácil e rápido acessar os recursos deste projeto.

1 Faça a ativação dos códigos dos seus livros.

Se você NÃO tem cadastro na plataforma:

- acesse o endereço <**login.smaprendizagem.com**>;
- na parte inferior da tela, clique em "Registre-se" e depois no botão "Alunos";
- escolha o país;
- preencha o formulário com os dados do tutor, do aluno e de acesso.

O seu tutor receberá um *e-mail* para validação da conta. Atenção: sem essa validação, não é possível acessar a plataforma.

Se você JÁ tem cadastro na plataforma:

- em seu computador, acesse a plataforma pelo endereço <**login.smaprendizagem.com**>;
- em seguida, você visualizará os livros que já estão ativados em seu perfil. Clique no botão "Códigos ou licenças", insira o código abaixo e clique no botão "Validar".

Este é o seu código de ativação! →

DX11L-2TJBR-AE8KP

CB074531

2 Acesse os recursos

usando um computador.

No seu navegador de internet, digite o endereço <**login.smaprendizagem.com**> e acesse sua conta. Você visualizará todos os livros que tem cadastrados. Para escolher um livro, basta clicar na sua capa.

usando um dispositivo móvel.

Instale o aplicativo **SM Aprendizagem**, que está disponível gratuitamente na loja de aplicativos do dispositivo. Utilize o mesmo *login* e a mesma senha que você cadastrou na plataforma.

Importante! Não se esqueça de sempre cadastrar seus livros da SM em seu perfil. Assim, você garante a visualização dos seus conteúdos, seja no computador, seja no dispositivo móvel. Em caso de dúvida, entre em contato com nosso canal de atendimento pelo **telefone 0800 72 54876** ou pelo ***e-mail* atendimento@grupo-sm.com**.

205240_7746

sm

LIVRO LEARNING TOGETHER 5 F1 LA ED 2021

LEARNING TOGETHER

BOOK 5

ENGLISH

LUCIANA RENDA B. DE MELO
Graduada em Pedagogia e Administração de Empresas.
Pós-graduada em Psicopedagogia e Linguística Aplicada a Língua Inglesa.
Diploma de Ensino de Inglês pelo SIT (School for International Training).
Professora de Inglês e pedagoga bilíngue.

MARCELO BACCARIN
Mestre em Educação.
Graduado em Pedagogia (Orientação Educacional) e Letras: Inglês-Português.
Diploma em Ensino de Inglês como Língua Estrangeira (DTEFLA) pela Universidade de Cambridge.
Professor, coordenador e gestor na rede particular de ensino.
Formador de professores e consultor independente em educação e bilinguismo.

RONALDO LIMA JR.
Doutor em Linguística.
Mestre em Linguística Aplicada.
Graduado e Licenciado em Letras – Inglês.
Professor do Departamento de Estudos da Língua Inglesa da Universidade Federal do Ceará.

ENSINO FUNDAMENTAL

São Paulo, 2ª edição, 2021

sm

Learning Together 5

Direção editorial Cláudia Carvalho Neves
Gerência editorial Lia Monguilhott Bezerra
Gerência de *design* e produção André Monteiro
Edição executiva Ana Luiza Couto
Edição: Barbara Manholeti, Danuza Gonçalves
Assistência de edição: Natália Feulo do Espírito Santo
Suporte editorial: Fernanda de Araújo Fortunato
Coordenação de preparação e revisão Cláudia Rodrigues do Espírito Santo
Preparação: Andréa Vidal
Revisão: Andréa Vidal
Coordenação de *design* Gilciane Munhoz
***Design*:** Thatiana Kalaes, Lissa Sakajiri
Coordenação de arte Andressa Fiorio
Edição de arte: Fernando Cesar Fernandes
Assistência de arte: Heidy Clemente, Rosangela Cesar de Lima
Assistência de produção: Leslie Morais
Coordenação de iconografia Josiane Laurentino
Pesquisa iconográfica: Ana Stein
Tratamento de imagem: Marcelo Casaro
Capa APIS Design
Ilustração da capa: Henrique Mantovani Petrus
Projeto gráfico APIS Design
Editoração eletrônica Estúdio Type
Pré-impressão Américo Jesus
Fabricação Alexander Maeda
Impressão Ricargraf

Em respeito ao meio ambiente, as folhas deste livro foram produzidas com fibras obtidas de árvores de florestas plantadas, com origem certificada.

Dados Internacionais de Catalogação na Publicação (CIP)
(Câmara Brasileira do Livro, SP, Brasil)

Melo, Luciana Renda B. de
Learning together, 5º ano : ensino fundamental / Luciana Renda B. de Melo, Marcelo Baccarin, Ronaldo Lima Jr.. — 2. ed. — São Paulo : Edições SM, 2021. — (Learning together)

ISBN 978-65-5744-278-4 (aluno)
ISBN 978-65-5744-308-8 (professor)

1. Inglês (Ensino fundamental) I. Baccarin, Marcelo. II. Lima Junior, Ronaldo. III. Título. IV. Série.

21-66441 CDD-372.652

Índice para catálogo sistemático:

1. Inglês : Ensino fundamental 372.652

Cibele Maria Dias — Bibliotecária — CRB-8/9427

2ª edição, 2021
3ª impressão 2023

SM Educação
Rua Cenno Sbrighi, 25 - Edifício West Tower n. 45 - 1º andar
Água Branca 05036-010 São Paulo SP Brasil
Tel. 11 2111-7400
atendimento@grupo-sm.com
www.grupo-sm.com/br

Apresentação

Caro(a) estudante,

Este livro foi cuidadosamente pensado para ajudar você a construir uma aprendizagem sólida e cheia de significados que lhe sejam úteis não somente hoje, mas também no futuro. Nele, você vai encontrar estímulos para criar, expressar ideias e pensamentos, refletir sobre o que aprende, trocar experiências e conhecimentos.

Os temas, os textos, as imagens e as atividades propostos neste livro oferecem oportunidades para que você se desenvolva como estudante e como cidadã(o), cultivando valores universais como responsabilidade, respeito, solidariedade, liberdade e justiça.

Acreditamos que é por meio de atitudes positivas e construtivas que se conquistam a autonomia e a capacidade para tomar decisões acertadas, resolver problemas e superar conflitos.

Esperamos que este material didático contribua para o seu desenvolvimento e para a sua formação.

Bons estudos!

Os autores

Conheça seu livro

Conhecer seu livro didático vai ajudá-lo(a) a aproveitar melhor as oportunidades de aprendizagem que ele oferece.

Este volume contém uma unidade inicial de seis páginas, oito unidades de oito páginas, duas revisões, um caderno de atividades e algumas seções especiais.

Veja como cada parte do seu livro está organizada.

Welcome
Summer Camp
HELPERS
FARM TIME

Abertura do livro

Welcome Unit

Você já deve ter algum conhecimento de inglês adquirido por meio de filmes, músicas, livros, programas de TV e pela internet. Nesta unidade, você terá a oportunidade de resgatar o que já sabe sobre a língua inglesa, além de perceber o quanto conhece sobre um dos idiomas mais usados no mundo.

Introdução da unidade

A unidade começa com uma história divertida que aborda temas do cotidiano de crianças da sua idade. A vida escolar, o ambiente familiar e a convivência entre amigos estão entre os assuntos que abrirão as portas para você aprender novas palavras, expressões orais e sons da língua inglesa.

UNIT
4
Having Fun
LUCAS

Desenvolvimento do assunto

Os textos, as imagens e as atividades destas páginas vão permitir que você compreenda o conteúdo que está sendo apresentado.

Time for text

Aqui você poderá ler textos relacionados ao tema da unidade e conhecer diferentes maneiras de se comunicar por meio da escrita.

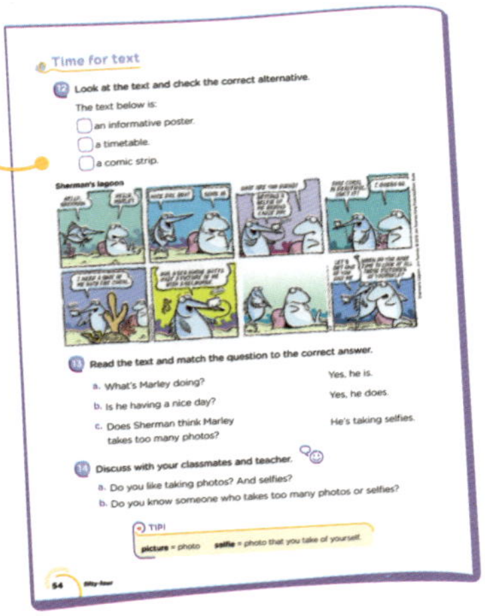

Time for text

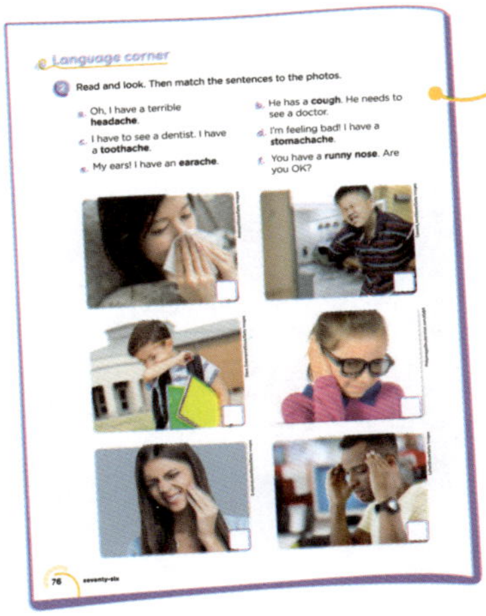
Language corner

2 Read and look. Then match the sentences to the photos.

a. Oh, I have a terrible **headache**.
b. He has a **cough**. He needs to see a doctor.
c. I have to see a dentist. I have a **toothache**.
d. I'm feeling bad! I have a **stomachache**.
e. My ears! I have an **earache**.
f. You have a **runny nose**. Are you OK?

76 seventy-six

Language corner

Alguns vocabulários da história de abertura serão apresentados e aprofundados em atividades que ajudarão você a falar, ouvir, ler e escrever em inglês.

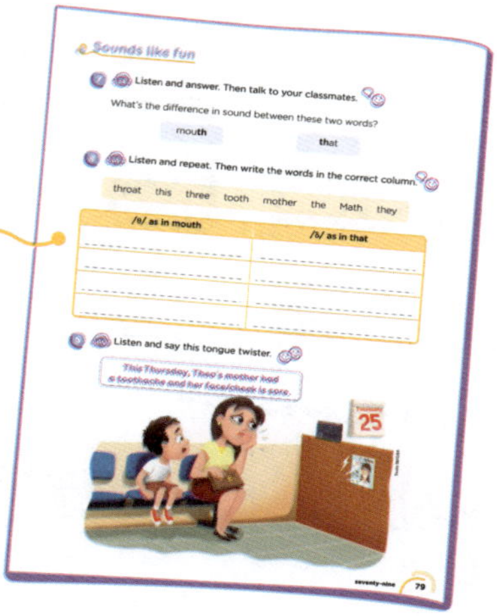
Sounds like fun

Listen and answer. Then talk to your classmates.

What's the difference in sound between these two words?

mouth that

Listen and repeat. Then write the words in the correct column.

throat this three tooth mother the Math they

/θ/ as in mouth	/ð/ as in that

Listen and say this tongue twister.

This Thursday, Theo's mother had a toothache and her face/cheek is sore.

seventy-nine 79

Sounds like fun

O conteúdo desta seção permitirá que você conheça os fonemas da língua inglesa. Ao realizar as atividades de áudio e pronúncia, você perceberá que falar inglês pode ser muito legal!

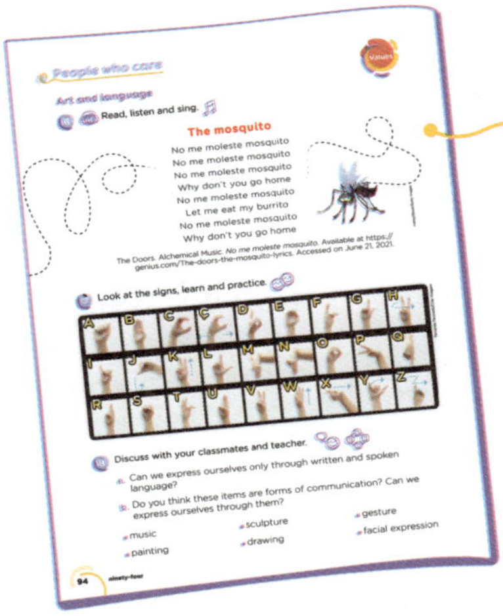
People who care

Art and language

Read, listen and sing.

The mosquito

No me moleste mosquito
No me moleste mosquito
No me moleste mosquito
Why don't you go home
No me moleste mosquito
Let me eat my burrito
No me moleste mosquito
Why don't you go home

Look at the signs, learn and practice.

Discuss with your classmates and teacher.

a. Can we express ourselves only through written and spoken language?
b. Do you think these items are forms of communication? Can we express ourselves through them?

music, sculpture, gesture, painting, drawing, facial expression

94 ninety-four

People who care

Este é o momento para refletir e conversar com os colegas sobre como ter boas práticas para melhorar a convivência com sua família, com a comunidade escolar e com todos a sua volta.

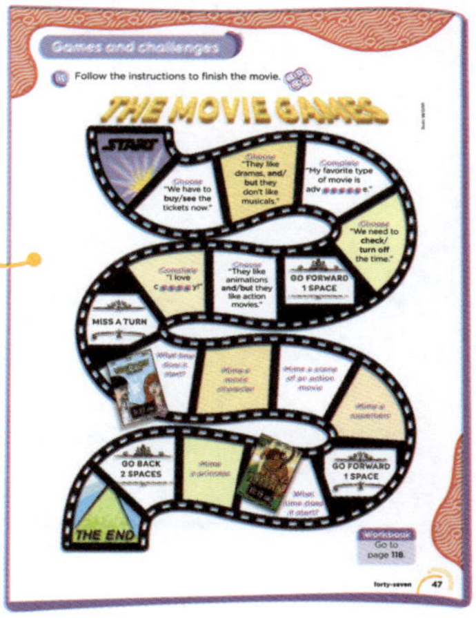
Games and challenges

Follow the instructions to finish the movie.

THE MOVIE GAMES

START ... MISS A TURN ... GO FORWARD 1 SPACE ... GO BACK 2 SPACES ... THE END

forty-seven 47

Games and challenges

Nesta página, você encontrará jogos para se divertir com os colegas, ao mesmo tempo que interage e resgata o que aprendeu na unidade.

Karaoke

Write the words. Then listen and complete the lyrics.

Who'll Stop the ______

Long as I remember,
The ______ been comin' down
______ of mystery pourin'
Confusion on the ground.
Good men through the ages
Tryin' to find the ______
And I wonder,
Still I wonder
Who'll stop the ______

I went down Virginia,
Seekin' shelter from the ______
Caught up in the fable,
I watched the tower grow
Five-year plans and new deals
Wrapped in golden chains
And I wonder,
Still I wonder
Who'll stop the ______

Heard the singers playin',
How we cheered for more.
The crowd had rushed together
Tryin' to keep warm.
Still the ______ kept pourin',
Fallin' on my ears
And I wonder,
Still I wonder
Who'll stop the ______

112 one hundred and twelve

Karaoke

Aqui você conhece músicas em inglês que fazem parte da cultura *pop*. Divirta-se cantando em inglês com a turma toda!

Finalizando o capítulo

No fim de algumas unidades, há seções que buscam ampliar seus conhecimentos sobre a leitura de imagens, a diversidade cultural e os conteúdos abordados.

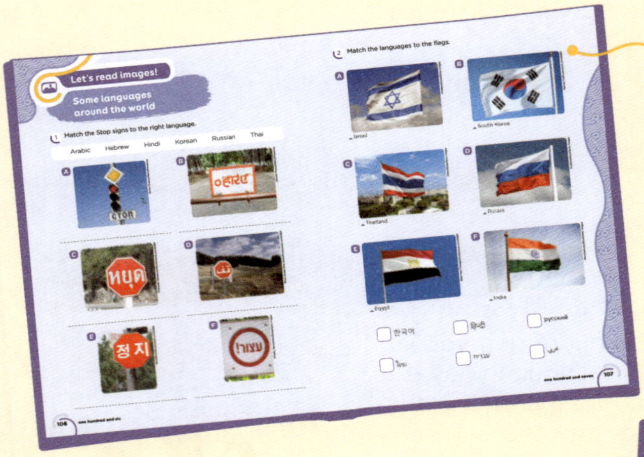
Let's read images!
Some languages around the world

Let's read images!

Nesta seção você vai apreciar e analisar imagens para ampliar seu repertório cultural.

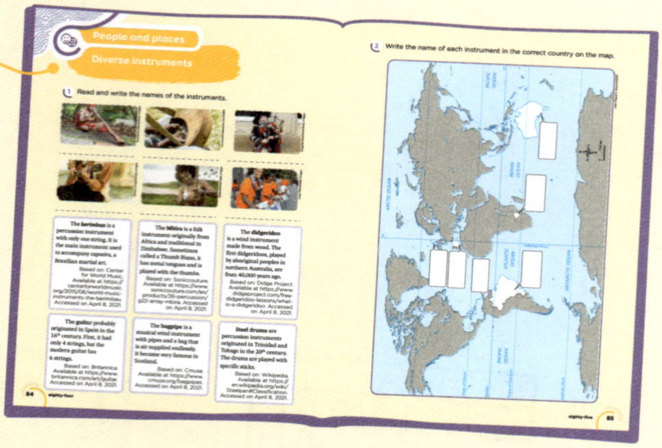
People and places
Diverse instruments

People and places

Esta seção leva você a conhecer algumas características culturais de diferentes comunidades.

Ao fim do livro

Glossary

Glossary

Você poderá consultar o glossário quando sentir dificuldade em compreender alguma palavra ou expressão usada no livro, ou sempre que quiser relembrar algum conteúdo estudado.

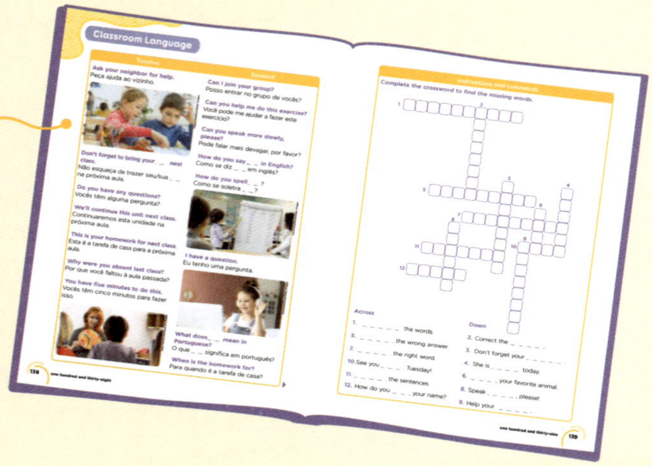
Classroom Language

Classroom language

Consulte esta seção para se comunicar em inglês com todos na sala de aula.

Follow-up

Este espaço permite que você revise o que aprendeu nas últimas quatro unidades. Com as atividades desta seção, você poderá avaliar se há algum tema a ser aperfeiçoado e também acompanhar seu desenvolvimento nas aulas de inglês.

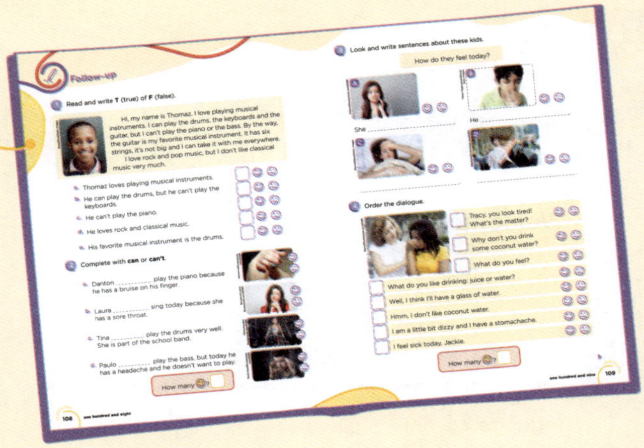
Follow-up
Read and write T (true) or F (false).
Complete with can or can't.
Look and write sentences about these kids.
How do they feel today?
Order the dialogue.
How many

Projects

Nesta seção, você realizará projetos em grupo relacionados aos temas das unidades. Essa é uma boa oportunidade para aprender a conversar, ouvir e compartilhar experiências e ideias com os(as) colegas.

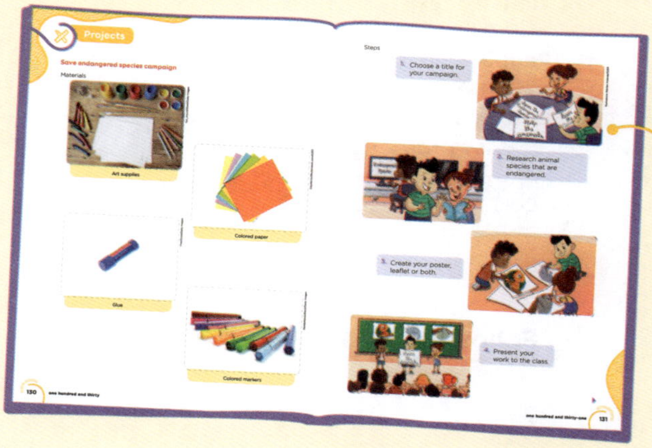
Projects
Save endangered species campaign
Materials
Steps
1. Choose a title for your campaign.
2. Research animal species that are endangered.
3. Create your poster, leaflet or both.
4. Present your work to the class.

Workbook

Este é um caderno de atividades que contém desafios especialmente elaborados para cada unidade estudada. Você poderá utilizá-lo em sala de aula ou como lição de casa.

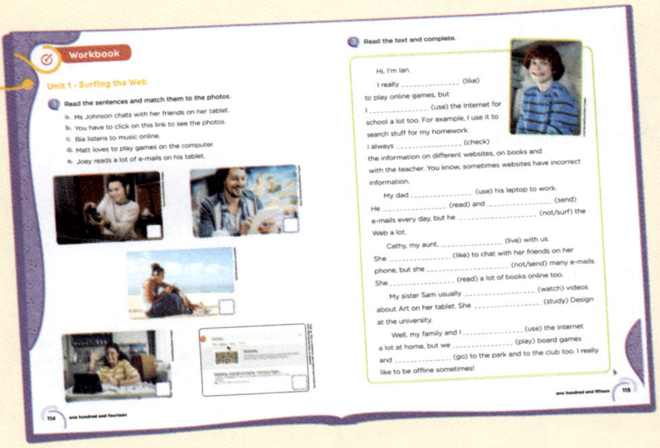
Workbook
Unit 1 - Surfing the Web
Read the sentences and match them to the photos.
Read the text and complete.

ÍCONES USADOS NO LIVRO

Atividade em dupla

Atividade em grupo

Atividade oral

Roda de conversa

Áudio
Indica a faixa de áudio relacionada à atividade.

Música
Indica que há uma música relacionada à atividade.

Karaoke
Indica que há uma versão karaokê da canção explorada na seção *Karaoke*.

Destacar
Indica que há um destacável no final do livro para ser utilizado na atividade.

Colar
Indica que há adesivos no final do livro para utilização na atividade.

Values
Indica a seção *People who care*.

OED
Indica que há um Objeto Educacional Digital a ser explorado no livro digital.

Summary

CLASS

Mauro Souza/ID/BR

Rafael Rodriz/ID/BR

André Santos/ID/BR

Wilson's Summer Camp
LET ME TELL YOU ABOUT THE ACTIVITIES YOU CAN DO AT WILSON'S SUMMER CAMP. YOU CAN DO JUDO, ________________ OR EVEN PLAY SOCCER OR ________________.
EXERCISE TIME
WOW! I WANT TO DO EVERYTHING.
WHAT ABOUT FEEDING ________________ OR PICKING FRUIT AND VEGETABLES?
I LOVE ANIMALS.
FARM TIME
I WANT TO ________________ FRUIT.

THESE ARE SOME OF THE ______ THAT WILL HELP YOU THESE DAYS. SO LET'S START THE DAY AND HAVE LOTS OF FUN!
HELPERS
MAURICIO COOK
JOÃO NURSE
VALDO
DIANA
CLEANERS
YEAH!
Everton Caetano/ID/BR

Welcome

Summer Camp

1 02 Look, listen and complete. Then act out.

people	*capoeira*	
animals	pick	volleyball

2 Read the dialogue and answer.

a. Where are the kids?

They are in a

______________________.

b. What can they do there?

They can do ______________,

judo, play ______________

and ______________.

c. Who are some of the people that work in the summer camp?

Maurício is a cook, João is a

______________, Valdo and

Diana are ______________.

3 Look, answer and draw.

a. What are they doing?

Fred Sweet/Shutterstock.com/ID/BR

They're ______________________.
(skateboard)

b. What's he doing?

Digitalskillet/iStock/Getty Images

He's ______________________
a book. (read)

c. What's he doing?

Predrag Vuckovic/iStock/Getty Images

____
a mountain. (climb)

d. What's she doing?

Konstantin Shishkin/iStock/Getty Images

______________________.
(ski)

e. What are they doing?

MBI/iStock/Getty Images

______________________.
(eat)

f. What's she doing?

Imgorthand/iStock/Getty Images

____
her bike. (ride)

g. What are you doing?

I'm ______________________.

4 Look and stick.

Illustrations: Werllen Holanda/ID/BR

5 Look, read and check the sentences.

Raitan Ohi/ID/BR

a. ☐ There are pens under the table.

b. ☐ There is a lamp beside the armchair.

c. ☐ There is a TV in the living room.

d. ☐ There are some toys behind the sofa.

e. ☐ There is a teddy bear under the box.

Conteúdo na versão digital

6 Look, read and answer the questions.

A

Does she play tennis?

______________________________.

B

Does he have a rabbit?

______________________________.

C

Do they go to school by bike?

______________________________.

D

Do you like fruit?

______________________________.

7 Look, reorder and write.

A

live / I / Brazil / in

______________________________.

B

to / school / ride / You / bike / your

______________________________.

C

at / Mary / up / o'clock / wakes / 7

______________________________.

D

like / They / apples

______________________________.

8 Play and tell.

START
FAVORITE COLOR
TIME I WAKE UP
FAVORITE SPORT
SOMETHING I LIKE ABOUT SCHOOL
FAVORITE SEASON
SOMETHING I LIKE TO DO
HOW I GET TO SCHOOL
PLACE WHERE I AM FROM
FAVORITE FOOD
TIME I GO TO BED
SUPER
SOMETHING A FRIEND LIKES
FAVORITE PLACE
SOMETHING FUN YOU DO IN SUMMER
FAVORITE ANIMAL
END

Rodrigo Arraya/ID/BR

UNIT 1 Surfing the Web

1 (03) Look, listen and read. Then act out.

HI, I'M JIM, AND THIS IS MY MOM, DEBBIE. SHE WORKS ON THE COMPUTER. I THINK SHE READS AND SENDS MESSAGES ALL DAY!
I'M FINISHING HERE, JIM. LET'S GO FOR A WALK LATER.

MY SISTER, CARLY, LOVES TO READ. SHE KEEPS A CHANNEL IN WHICH SHE POSTS VIDEOS ABOUT THE BOOKS SHE READS. SHE'S A BOOKWORM.

Ronaldo Barata/ID/BR

THIS IS MY DAD, QUICO. HE LIKES TO COOK RECIPES HE FINDS ONLINE. HE COOKS VERY WELL AND DOESN'T USUALLY NEED HELP.
HEY, JIMMY, DINNER IS ALMOST READY.
THIS IS MY UNCLE, TEO. LET'S TAKE A PICTURE OF HIM PLAYING BASKETBALL. HE PLAYS IT VERY WELL!
SHARE THIS PHOTO WITH ME, JAMES. IT'S FOR MY SOCIAL MEDIA.
JAMES, JIMMY, JIM... WHY DO PEOPLE CALL ME ALL THESE NAMES? WELL, LET'S SEARCH!
Search
10

Language corner

2 (04) Read, complete and listen.

Beatriz Frederico Deborah Carla Leonard Joseph

A

Kupicoo/iStock/Getty Images

My name is ______________, but people call me Debbie, Debby or Debra.

B

Shapecharge/iStock/Getty Images

His name is ______________, but people call him Joey or Joe.

C

Jani Bryson/iStock/Getty Images

This is ______________, but you can call her Carly or Carlie.

D
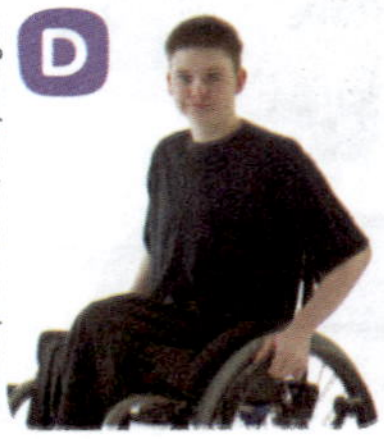
Christopher Futcher/Getty Images

My name is ______________, but I have two nicknames: Leo and Lenny.

E

Laflor/iStock/Getty Images

I'm ______________, but people call me Bia.

F

DRB Images, LLC/iStock/Getty Images

This is ______________, but people call him Quico.

3 Look, read and circle the **name** or the **nickname**.

A

NICOLE/NICKY, PLEASE, ANSWER NUMBER 2.
Wavebreakmedia/iStock/Getty Images

B

MR RONALD SULLIVAN/ RON, COME IN, PLEASE.
MBI/iStock/Getty Images

C

SO, CAROLINE/ CAROL, ARE YOU HUNGRY?
Skynesher/iStock/Getty Images

D

LOOK AT THAT GOAL, MATTHEW/MATT.
Prostock-Studio/iStock/Getty Images

4 Read and complete the sentences.

games	file	Web	information	movies	messages

Downloading... 50%
Nixxphotography/iStock/Getty Images

a. Download and save the ______________ to open it.

GAME JUNGLE
NEW GAME
SETTINGS
Boris Panov/iStock/Getty Images

b. My brother always plays online ______________ with his friends.

Andrey_Popov/Shutterstock.com/ID/BR

c. I use the Internet to search for ______________.

COMPOSE
Inbox (1)
Important
RayaHristova/iStock/Getty Images

d. My dad sends and receives ______________ all day.

http://www.
Rvlsoft/iStock/Getty Images

e. My friend Mike uses his tablet to surf the ______________.

Andrey_Popov/Shutterstock.com/ID/BR

f. I watch online ______________ and videos on the laptop.

5 05 Listen, ask and answer.

WHAT DO YOU DO ONLINE?
I STUDY AND DO MY HOMEWORK. BUT I LISTEN TO MUSIC AND PLAY GAMES, TOO.
Steve Debenport/iStock/Getty Images

6 Read, listen and circle.

Grady Reese/iStock/Getty Images

I use the Internet for school.

Cathy Yeulet/iStock/Getty Images

Pam searches for information about her name.

Antoniodiaz/Shutterstock.com/ID/BR

She reads and **sends** messages all day.

Conteúdo na versão digital

Blackcat/iStock/Getty Images

Cathy's video channel is very interesting. **It contains** information about books.

DragonImages/iStock/Getty Images

Dad watches videos online.

We usually add **-s** or **-es** to the verbs after **he**/**I**, **she**/**you** and **it**/**we**.

7 Read and complete.

Language Summary

I You We They	**click** on the link. **watch** videos.	He She It	**uses** the Internet for school. **searches** for an address. **contains** information about books.
I You We They	**don't listen** to music. **don't search** for information.	He She It	**doesn't send** e-mails. **doesn't watch** movies. **doesn't contain** information about games.

a. Pam ____________ a lot of messages every day. (send)

b. My best friend ____________ to rock and roll, but I ____________ to pop music. (listen)

c. My father ____________ online games because he doesn't like them. (not/play)

d. When I don't know something, I ____________ for it online. (search)

e. We need to be careful when we ____________ the Web. (surf)

f. I ____________ to read books online. I prefer their print version. (not/like)

TIP!

don't = do not

doesn't = does not

Sounds like fun

8 (07) Listen, match and say.

[æ]
bad

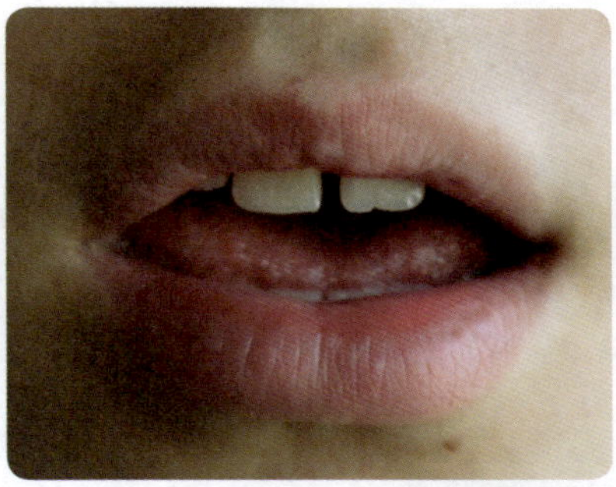

HNfotos/ID/BR

[ɛ]
bed

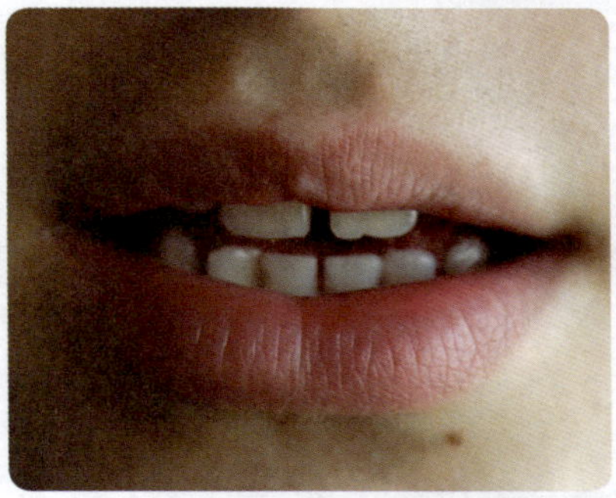

HNfotos/ID/BR

Pat

Matt

Beth

Jeff

Brad

Greg

9 (08) Listen, circle and sing.

She Loves You

She says she loves you,
And you know that can't be bad,
She says she loves you,
And you know you should be glad
She loves you, yeh, yeh, yeh,
She loves you, yeh, yeh, yeh,
And with a love like that,
You know you should be glad

Pavel K/shutterstock.com/ID/BR
VikaSuh/vectorstock.com/ID/BR

John Lennon; Paul McCartney. *She Loves You*. Available at https://www.thebeatles.com/song/she-loves-you. Accessed on May 25, 2021.

Time for text

10 Read the text and check the correct alternative.

http://pbskids.org/itsmylife/friends/nicknames

FRIENDS | GAMES | VIDEO | ADVICE | CELEBS | BLOG

What to do with a Bad Nickname

It's usually okay when people call us by a positive nickname. But when classmates choose a cruel nickname, it's difficult to get them to stop. What do you do, then?

Ask your friends to be nice.
If the kids using the nicknames are your friends, tell them how bad it makes you feel. Maybe you did something silly and your friends have started calling you "x". Is that a problem for you? Well, if it is, tell them! Explain that you don't want to be called "x", and if they're really your friends, they'll understand.
If the kids are not your friends, speak to an adult (your mom or dad, your teacher or school counsellor) about this. They will do something to protect you.

Tangente Design/ID/BR

Based on PBS KIDS. *Nicknames: Ditching Bad Nicknames*.
Available at http://r53-vip-soup.pbskids.org/itsmylife/friends/nicknames/article5.html.
Accessed on May 18, 2021.

The text is about:

☐ positive and negative use of nicknames. ☐ popular nicknames.

11 Read the text again and complete the sentences.

don't like | like | makes | doesn't use

a. We usually ____________________ positive nicknames.

b. A cruel nickname ____________________ you feel bad.

c. Tell your friends if you ____________________ the nickname.

d. A real friend ____________________ cruel nicknames.

12 Read and stick. Then complete the sentences.

search engine website	**results page**	**website with the information**

a. I visit a ______________________________ to look for some information.

b. The ______________________________ shows links to websites.

c. I have to click on the link to access the ______________________________
______________________________.

13 Discuss with your classmates and teacher.

a. Do you like the text on page 22? Is the information important?

b. Do you like all your nicknames? Which ones do you like?

Conteúdo na versão digital

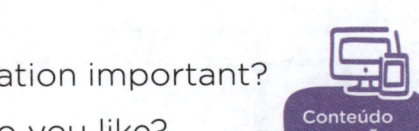

14 Research the origin of your name or family name.

- Visit a search engine website and type some key words. For example, "Ana origin name"; "Ferreira origin name".
- Choose one or more websites with the information you want.
- Write some of your research results in your notebook.
- Share your information with the class.

TIP!

Some websites have fake information (information that is not true). So, it is important to check what you read on other websites, in books and talk to people. Information from important institutions, universities (.edu), organizations (.org) and government authorities (.gov) is usually correct.

People who care

Values

Internet safety tips

15 Read the text and stick.

Don't share your personal information (name, address, school name, telephone number) without your parents' permission.

Don't include your real name or birthday on your username.

Don't share your passwords with anyone. Only your parents need to know your passwords.

Don't post photos or videos without your parents' permission.

Don't arrange to meet someone you met online in person.

Talk to your parents before you download apps. A virus may infect your computer.

Don't send or respond to insulting messages. Tell your parents if you receive one. If something happens online that makes you feel uncomfortable, talk to your parents or to your teacher at school.

Many social networking websites have a minimum age to sign up. This is to protect you!

Based on The New York Public Library. *Internet Safety Tips for Children and Teens*. Available at https://www.nypl.org/help/about-nypl/legal-notices/internet-safety-tips. Accessed on May 17, 2021.

16 Discuss with your classmates.

a. Do you think these Internet safety tips are useful?

b. Think about other tips and share them with your classmates.

Games and challenges

17 Read and complete the crossword puzzle.

1
2
3
4
5
6
7
8

Workbook
Go to page **114**.

ACROSS

1. Playing online ______________________ is my favorite activity.

3. My dad searches ______________________ for new recipes.

7. There are different ______________________ engine websites.

8. My mom reads and sends ______________________ all day.

DOWN

2. I don't ______________________ personal information on social media.

4. I love my ______________________. Everybody calls me Fran.

5. My sister keeps a video ______________________ with many followers.

6. Only share your ______________________ with your parents.

UNIT 2 Pictures of the Wildlife

1 09 Look, listen and act out.

HI, EVERYONE. DAN, WHAT PHOTO IS THAT?
HI, ALYSSA. IT'S A SNAKE! VERY COOL, HUH? I LOVE REPTILES. DO YOU KNOW THAT SNAKES OFTEN CHANGE THEIR SKIN?
REALLY?! I LOVE BIRDS! LOOK, THIS IS A BLUE MACAW.
THAT'S BEAUTIFUL!
THAT'S INTERESTING! BUT I PREFER CYNTHIA'S PHOTO. WHAT'S THAT, CYNTHIA? IT'S SO BEAUTIFUL!
OH, THIS IS A HUMMINGBIRD. CAN YOU BELIEVE THAT HUMMINGBIRDS SOMETIMES VISIT MORE THAN 1,000 FLOWERS IN ONE DAY?
YES. IT'S A BRAZILIAN BIRD AND IT'S ENDANGERED.

EXACTLY. IT SAYS HERE THAT BLUE MACAWS CAN DISAPPEAR COMPLETELY.
OH, THAT'S SAD!
YES. OTHER ANIMALS ARE ENDANGERED TOO, LIKE POLAR BEARS, HIPPOS, LIONS...
UH... WE HAVE NO HOMEWORK FOR TOMORROW, RIGHT?
WRONG! WE HAVE A PRESENTATION ABOUT BIRDS AND REPTILES, REMEMBER?
OH, NO! BYE, GUYS... I HAVE TO FINISH MY PROJECT ABOUT SNAKES.
Everton Caetano/ID/BR

Language corner

Conteúdo na versão digital

2 (10) Look, read and match. Then listen.

MartinMaritz/Shutterstock.com/ID/BR

hippo ☐

Tane Mahuta/iStock/Getty Images

jaguar ☐

Andrew Jalbert/Shutterstock.com/ID/BR

sea turtle ☐

ShaneGross/iStock/Getty Images

shark ☐

Belizar73/iStock/Getty Images

armadillo ☐

Dirk Freder/iStock/Getty Images

bear ☐

Maciej Czekajewski/Shutterstock.com/ID/BR

macaw ☐

Kjersti Joergensen/iStock/Getty Images

monkey ☐

Kungverylucky/Shutterstock.com/ID/BR

sloth ☐

a. This mammal is small. It can make holes in the ground or can roll into a ball.

b. This big mammal lives in cold places and usually sleeps all winter.

c. This reptile has a carapace round its body and lives in the sea.

d. This big mammal lives on land and in the water.

e. This big cat usually has spots on its body.

f. This mammal usually lives in trees and has a common ancestor with humans.

g. This fish lives in oceans and can be very dangerous.

h. This mammal lives in trees and is very slow.

i. This bird is colorful and noisy and has a long tail.

Sources: Rainforest Alliance. Available at https://www.rainforest-alliance.org/; The IUCN Red List of Threatened Species. Available at https://www.iucnredlist.org/. Accessed on June 16, 2021.

3 (11) Read, listen and say.

IT'S A BIG MAMMAL THAT LIVES IN THE OCEAN.

IT'S A WHALE.

PaulWolf/iStock/Getty Images

4 Look, read and write **T** (true) or **F** (false).

Language Summary

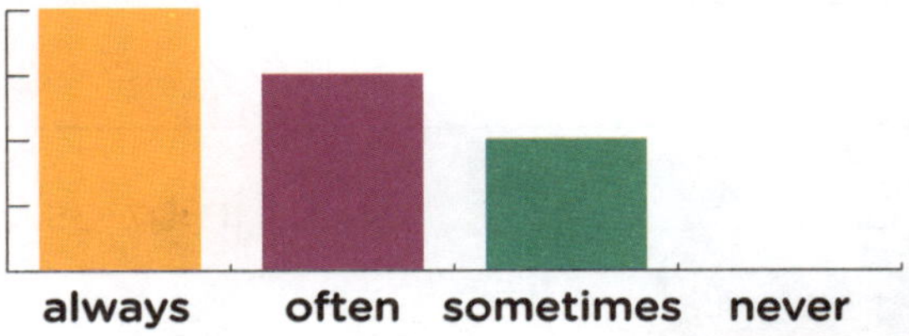
always
often
sometimes
never

A

Matthew Hart/iStock/Getty Images

B

Invisiblewl/iStock/Getty Images

C

Josef Friedhuber/iStock/Getty Images

D

PaigePam/iStock/Getty Images

a. ☐ Jaguars **never** swim.

b. ☐ Lions **sometimes** climb trees.

c. ☐ Capybaras **often** live in groups.

d. ☐ Monkeys **always** live in trees.

5 Read and complete with **always**, **often**, **sometimes** or **never**.

The diet of some animals

capybaras	monkeys	armadillos	polar bears
vegetables	meat / vegetables	meat / vegetables	meat

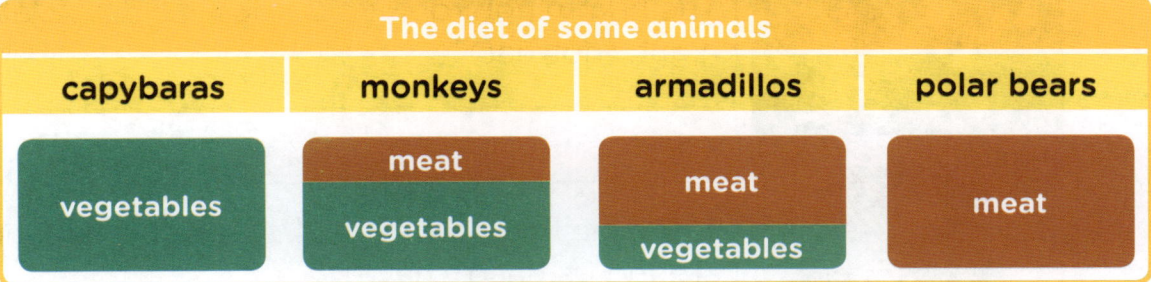

a. Polar bears ________________ eat vegetables.

b. Armadillos ________________ eat vegetables.

c. Capybaras ________________ eat vegetables.

d. Monkeys ________________ eat vegetables.

6 Look, read and complete the sentences.

Language Summary	
The polar bear always **eats** meat. *It* always **eats** meat. *Polar bears* always **eat** meat. *They* always **eat** meat.	*The capybara* **doesn't eat** meat. *It* **doesn't eat** meat. *Capybaras* **don't eat** meat. *They* **don't eat** meat.
The jaguar **has** spots on its body. *Jaguars* **have** spots on its body.	*The turtle* **doesn't have** teeth. *Turtles* **don't have** teeth.

A
Ivkuzmin/iStock/Getty Images

The toucan always ______________________ in trees. (live)

B
Miroslav_1/iStock/Getty Images

Monkeys often ______________________ in trees. (live)

C
Matt Jeppson/Shutterstock.com/ID/BR

Most snakes ______________________ every day. (not/eat)

D
Mbolina/iStock/Getty Images

The hummingbird ______________________ at night. (not/eat)

E
GlobalP/iStock/Getty Images

The male lion ______________________ a mane around its head. (have)

F
MariSwanepoel/iStock/Getty Images

Female lions ______________________ a mane around their heads. (not/have)

Sounds like fun

7 (12) Read, listen and say.

Dirk Freder/iStock/Getty Images

Henrique NDR Martins/iStock/Getty Images

Orlandin/Shutterstock.com/ID/BR

m**a**caw

li**o**n

turtl**e**

8 (13) Listen to the sound /ə/. Circle and say.

Johannes Compaan/iStock/Getty Images

MikeLane45/iStock/Getty Images

Matt Gibson/iStock/Getty Images

Mahnken/iStock/Getty Images

capybara /ˌkæpɪˈbærə/

toucan /ˈtuːkən/

jaguar /ˈdʒægjuə(r)/

caiman /ˈkeɪmən/

9 (14) Listen and say.

The lion eats zebra
And the caiman, capybara
Can they trade their menus?
No. Why?
Cause the lion is in Africa
And the caiman, in America

ayoeb/vectorstock.com/ID/BR

Time for text

10 Read and stick.

http://www.brazilianwildlife.edu/facts

BRAZILIAN WILDLIFE – IMAGES AND FACTS

Home | Images and Facts | Animals A-Z | Helping animals

Toucans always live in small groups and nest in tree holes. The toucan likes to keep its house clean and tidy. It never brings any dried plants or any other objects into their homes. Toucans are not at risk of extinction, but there is a reduction in their population.

A toucan in a tree hole

When a macaw chooses his or her mate, they stay together for the rest of their lives. The couple is often seen taking care of each other. Some macaw species are seriously endangered because of the destruction of forests and the illegal capture.

A macaw couple

The golden lion tamarin eats fruit, insects, some flowers, some small reptiles, and small birds. Golden lions always share their food by offering it to others or by letting the others take part of it. They are endangered because of the destruction of their habitat and the illegal capture.

A golden lion tamarin feeding

The green turtle is a big, heavy sea turtle. It lives in tropical and subtropical waters. Females leave the sea to lay their eggs on the beach and they often choose the same beach where they were born. Green turtles are listed as an endangered species. They are illegally killed because of their meat and eggs.

Female green sea turtle laying eggs

Sources: National Geographic. Available at https://www.nationalgeographic.com/animals/birds/facts/toco-toucan?source=A-to-Z; https://www.nationalgeographic.com/animals/birds/facts/macaws?source=A-to-Z; https://www.nationalgeographic.com/animals/mammals/facts/golden-lion-tamarin; https://www.nationalgeographic.com/animals/reptiles/facts/green-sea-turtle; Neotropical Birds https://birdsoftheworld.org/bow/home. All sites accessed on June 16, 2021.

11 Read the text again and write the name of the animal.

a. The ______________________ shares its food.

b. The ______________________ lays eggs on the beach.

c. The ______________________ has a tidy nest.

d. The ______________________ takes care of its mate.

12 Read and circle the correct alternative.

a. Female green sea turtles **remember/don't remember** the place where they were born.

b. The golden lion tamarin **eats/doesn't eat** some small reptiles.

c. A toucan **brings/doesn't bring** dried plants into its nest.

d. A macaw **has/doesn't have** the same mate for life.

13 Discuss with your classmates and teacher.

a. Why are some animals endangered?

b. What can we do to change this? (You may use these words: protect, habitat, penalize, capture.)

c. What do you think can be done to stop this situation?

14 Choose a photo of a wild animal and write a caption.

- Choose a wild animal.
- Research and complete the sentences about the animal.

It's ______________________________.

It lives ______________________________.

It eats ______________________________.

It has ______________________________.

It ______________________________.

- Choose a photo or draw the animal.
- Write a short caption.

People who care

Protecting wildlife

15 Read and match the titles to the sentences.

What you can do to protect wildlife

You are part of the web of life.

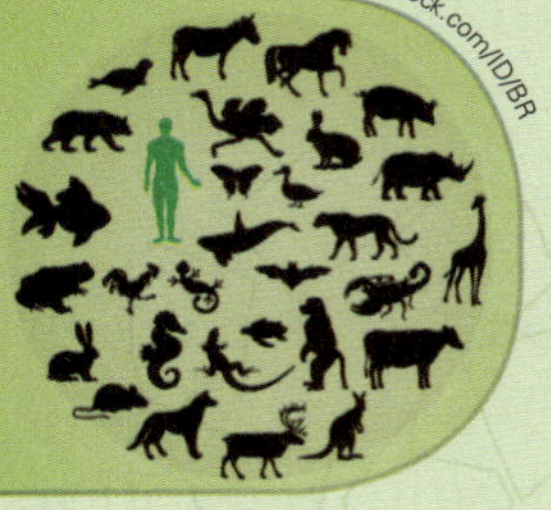

Desdemona72/Shutterstock.com/ID/BR

Learn more about endangered species.

Don't buy or keep wild animals.

Create a place for wildlife in your backyard.

Learn about plants and animals that need special protection. Share the information you learn with your family and friends.

This includes anything from frogs and turtles to exotic birds.

Remember that everything you do has an effect on dolphins, birds, monkeys, jaguars, etc.

Plant a tree with fruits that birds like.

Adapted from Marcia Lesky. *Wild Animals That Need Our Help*. Available at https://defenders.org/publications/kids-sea-otter-coloring-page. Accessed on June 16, 2021.

16 Search online and talk to your classmates and teacher.

a. An endangered animal.

b. The importance of that animal.

c. What you can do to protect that animal and the environment.

17 Spot the seven mistakes.

Werllen Holanda/ID/BR

Workbook
Go to page **116**.

People and places

Some interesting jobs

1 Who says what? Read and write the names William, David, Eugene and Sandra in the correct lines.

a. ______________________ works with fish.

b. ______________________ saves whales that are stuck on the beach.

c. ______________________ words to save endangered species.

d. ______________________ has had accidents with snakes.

Tony Karumba/AFP/Getty Images

Hi. My name is William and I am a herpetologist. A what? A person who studies reptiles and amphibians. In my case, I study snakes. I extract their venom every day so that we can make venom antiserum. Is it dangerous? Oh, yes! I have been bitten a few times in my life.

Hi. I am David. I am a wildlife veterinarian. I specialize in marine mammals, that is whales, seals, sea lions and dolphins. My work is to help animals that have come ashore and cannot go back, because they are sick, or accidentally got stuck or other reasons.

Marty Melville/AFP/Getty Images

Molishka/Shutterstock.com/ID/BR

Hello there! My name is Eugene and I am a wildlife biologist. I work for the federal government of my country studying ecosystems and trying to save endangered species. I must study a lot, and I love my job, because I know that I am helping the planet.

Hi. I am Sandra and I am an ichthyologist. This is a complicated name for someone who dedicates their life to fish. I identify fish, observe their behaviors, and monitor the water quality where they live. I work at a university, so I must write and present papers on my studies.

Jens Köhler/Ullstein Bild/Getty Images

Based on https://explore.org/livecams. Accessed on April 8, 2021.

2 What other different jobs like these do you know?

____

____

____

3 Would you like to have one of these jobs? Which?

____

____

____

UNIT 3 Going to the Movies

1 🎧15 Look, listen and read. Then act out.

CineNow
tickets
I WANT TO SEE THE NEW *THE INVINCIBLES 4* MOVIE.
THE INVINCIBLES 4
CHARLIE the cat
I DON'T KNOW. I DON'T LIKE ACTION MOVIES. WHAT ABOUT *CHARLIE THE CAT*?
NO WAY! IT'S A MOVIE FOR BABIES!
IT'S NOT! IT'S A DRAMA ABOUT A GIRL AND HER CAT.
THE INVINCIBLES 4
CHARLIE the cat
COME ON, KIDS. WE HAVE TO DECIDE WHICH MOVIE TO SEE AND CHECK THE SESSION TIMES.

The Invincibles 4
2:10 pm - 4:20 pm - 7:00 pm
Charlie: The Cat
2:15 pm - 4:30 pm - 7:10 pm
The Distant Galaxy
2:45 pm - 5:10 pm - 7:30 pm
WELL, IT'S ____________ AND *THE INVINCIBLES 4* STARTS AT ____________. *CHARLIE THE CAT* STARTS AT ____________.
WE NEED TO BUY THE TICKETS FIRST AND THERE'S A LONG LINE. SO, WE HAVE TO CHOOSE ANOTHER MOVIE.
THE DISTANT GALAXY
LET ME SEE... WHAT ABOUT *THE DISTANT GALAXY*?
GREAT! I LIKE SCI-FI MOVIES AND IT STARTS AT ____________. WE HAVE TIME TO BUY POPCORN AND JUICE!
THE DISTANT GALAXY 3D
LOOK, WE NEED TO PUT ON 3D GLASSES.
YEAH! LET'S BUY THE TICKETS FIRST AND THEN WE CAN BUY THE POPCORN, OK?
POPCORN
CINENOW

Designed by rawpixel/Freepik

Raitan Ohi/ID/BR

2 Listen and write the times.

Language corner

3 16 Look, read and match. Then listen.

A
Tyler Olson/Shutterstock.com/ID/BR

B
5
Tyler Olson/Shutterstock.com/ID/BR

C
Lizardflms/Shutterstock.com/ID/BR

D
Catherine Yeulet/iStock/Getty Images

E
MAX
THEATRE
Slobo/iStock/Getty Images

F
Vgajic/iStock/Getty Images

G
Pimpan/Shutterstock.com/ID/BR

H
Steve Debenport/iStock/Getty Images

- [ ] We have to **buy the tickets** now.
- [ ] Let's **go to the movies**!
- [ ] I want to **buy popcorn and juice**.
- [ ] **See the movie** and enjoy it!
- [ ] Let me **choose the film**.
- [ ] We need to **check the session times**.
- [ ] Please, **turn off your cell phone**.
- [ ] We have to **put on 3D glasses** to see this movie.

4 Read the sentences again and complete. Then talk to a classmate.

First I ______________________________, then

I ______________________________, after that

I ______________________________.

5 Look, read and complete with the movie genre.

action | adventure | drama | comedy | musical | animation | sci-fi

DOG DAYS
DIARY of a Wimpy Kid

Twentieth Century Fox Film Corporation/Everett Collection/Fotoarena

Diary of a Wimpy Kid: Dog Days

Genre: comedy, adventure

School's out and Greg is on vacation. But something can go wrong. *Wimpy Kid* brings good messages with humor.

THE SOUND of MUSIC

20th Century Fox/ID/BR

The Sound of Music

Genre: ______________________

____

A woman leaves the convent and goes to work in a house taking care of seven children. Good movie with glorious music.

JACK BLACK
KUNG FU PANDA
2

DreamWorks Animation/ID/BR

Kung Fu Panda 2

Genre: ______________________

____

Po and his friends fight to stop a villain from taking control of China.

E.T.

Universal Pictures/Everett Collection/Fotoarena

E.T.: The Extra-Terrestrial

Genre:

____

A dramatic and exciting story about a boy who helps his alien friend to return to his planet.

Based on Common Sense Media. *Diary of a Wimpy Kid*: Dog Days. Available at: https://www.commonsensemedia.org/movie-reviews/diary-of-a-wimpy-kid-dog-days; *The Sound of Music*. Available at: https://www.commonsensemedia.org/movie-reviews/the-sound-of-music; *Kung Fu Panda*. Available at https://www.commonsensemedia.org/movie-reviews/kung-fu-panda; *E.T.: The Extra-Terrestrial*. Available at https://www.commonsensemedia.org/movie-reviews/et-the-extra-terrestrial. Accessed on: May 19, 2021.

6 (17) Read, listen and interview your classmates.

Language Summary

What kind of movies **do**	you / they	**like**?	**I like** action movies, *but* I **don't like** sci-fi. **We like** comedies *and* adventures. **They like** dramas, *but* they **don't like** musicals.
What kind of movies **does**	she / he	**like**?	She **likes** animation, *but* she **doesn't like** comedies. He **likes** musicals *and* dramas.

WHAT KIND OF MOVIES DO YOU LIKE?

Jacek Chabraszewski/Shutterstock.com/ID/BR

I LIKE COMEDIES, BUT I DON'T LIKE SCI-FI.

7 Read and check the correct alternative.

Language Summary

What time does { **the movie** start? / **it** end?	**The film starts** / **It ends** } at 3:15. / 5:05.

http://www.landmarkcinemas.com/london — **All film / All times**

ID/BR

Showtimes for **Tue 06/28/24 (today)** at London Megaplex

COCO

Walt Disney Pictures/Pixar Animation Studios/ID/BR

Coco

10:15 AM • 10:30 AM
12:10 PM • 1:10 PM • 3:45 PM

INSIDE OUT

Walt Disney Pictures/Pixar Animation Studios/ ID/BR

Inside Out

10:45 AM
12:20 PM • 3:50 PM • 6:40 PM

JOHNNY DEPP
WINONA RYDER
edward SCISSORHANDS

20th Century Fox/ID/BR

Edward Scissorhands

11:35 AM
1:45 PM • 4:10 PM • 6:20 PM

Based on IMDb. Available at https://www.imdb.com/. Accessed on May 18, 2021.

TIP!

a.m. = before noon **p.m.** = after noon

a. What time does the first session of *Coco* start?

It starts at:

- [ ] ten fifteen.
- [ ] three forty-five.
- [ ] noon.

b. What time does the last session of *Inside Out* start?

It starts at:

- [ ] ten forty-five.
- [ ] twelve twenty.
- [ ] six forty.

c. What time does the second session of *Edward Scissorhands* start?

It starts at:

- [ ] eleven thirty-five.
- [ ] one forty-five.
- [ ] four ten.

Sounds like fun

Conteúdo na versão digital

8 18 Listen, answer and say.

How many /**t**/ sounds can you hear in these questions?

a. What time?

b. What type?

9 19 Match, listen and say.

a. What time is it?	☐	It's a comedy.
b. What time does the movie start?	☐	It starts at 2:25 p.m.
c. What type of movie is it?	☐	Oh, yes, we love them!
d. Do you like action movies?	☐	It's 9:35 a.m.

10 20 Listen and sing.

BACK IN TIME

Tell me, doctor
Where are we going this time?
Is this the fifties?
Or nineteen ninety-nine?
All I wanted to do
Was play my guitar and sing

STEVEN SPIELBERG Presents
BACK TO THE FUTURE
A ROBERT ZEMECKIS Film
"BACK TO THE FUTURE"
MICHAEL J. FOX
CHRISTOPHER LLOYD · LEA THOMPSON · CRISPIN GLOVER
ROBERT ZEMECKIS & BOB GALE
ALAN SILVESTRI
BOB GALE
NEIL CANTON
STEVEN SPIELBERG KATHLEEN KENNEDY
FRANK MARSHALL
ROBERT ZEMECKIS

Amblin Entertainment/ Universal Pictures/ID/BR

John Victor Colla (CA); Christopher John Hayes (CA); Sean Thomas Hopper (CA); Huey Lewis (CA). Warner Chappel Edições Musicais LTDA. *Back in Time*. Available at https://genius.com/Huey-lewis-and-the-news-back-in-time-lyrics. Accessed on June 2, 2021.

Time for text

11 Read and answer the questions.

http://www.cinestarmovies.com/theaters

ID/BR

Cine Star ★★★★ FIND A MOVIE BY TITLE ▾ OR By city, State or ZIP code ▾

MY CINE STAR
Sign | Register
0 items in cart

HOME | MOVIES | THEATERS | CINEARTS | GIFT CARDS | VALUES | PRIVATE EVENTS | ABOUT

CINE STAR
Stevegeer/iStock/Getty Images

3005, Mark Street
Colorado
P 799-599-2172
F 799-599-2277

TODAY | SAT | SUN | MON | TUE | WED | THU | FRI

ALICE THROUGH THE LOOKING GLASS
Walt Disney Pictures/ID/BR

Alice Through the Looking Glass

IMAX – 3D

10:00 AM 12:50 PM 3:40 PM 6:40 PM

ZOOTOPIA
Walt Disney Animation Studios/ID/BR

Zootopia

IMAX – 3D

10:30 AM 11:50 AM 1:15 PM 2:50 PM 4:00 PM

Based on a movie theater website. Available at www.cinemark.com. Accessed on July 2, 2021.

a. What's the name of the movie theater? ______________________.

b. What's the address of the movie theater? ______________________.

c. What's the day of the week? ______________________.

d. What time does the first session of *Alice Through the Looking Glass* start? ______________________.

e. What time does the first session of *Zootopia* start in the afternoon? ______________________.

12 Read and write **T** (true) or **F** (false).

http://www.cinestarmovies/alicethroughthelookingglass

ID/BR

Alice Through the Looking Glass

Walt Disney Pictures/ID/BR

ALICE
LOOKING GLASS

Runtime: 108 min
Cast: Johnny Depp, Anne Hathaway, Mia Wasikowska, Rhys Ifans, Helena Bonham Carter, Sacha Baron Cohen, Alan Rickman, Stephen Fry, Michael Sheen, Timothy Spall
Genre: Fantasy, Adventure

Synopsis
Alice (Mia Wasikowska) returns to the funny world of Underland and travels back in time to save the Mad Hatter (Johnny Depp).

TODAY | SAT | SUN | MON | TUE | WED | THU | FRI

10:00 AM **12:50 PM** **3:40 PM** **6:40 PM**

Based on IMDb. Alice Through the Looking Glass. Available at https://www.imdb.com/title/tt2567026/?ref_=fn_al_tt_1. Accessed on May 18, 2021.

a. ☐ The movie is less than two hours (< 120 min) long.

b. ☐ The movie is a drama.

c. ☐ Mia Wasikowska and Johnny Depp are actors.

d. ☐ Alice is a character of the movie.

e. ☐ The synopsis is a short text that describes the story of the movie.

TIP!

character = a person in a film, book, etc.
actor = a man or boy who plays a character.
actress = a woman or girl who plays a character.
Example: Johnny Depp is an actor. Mad Hatter is his character.
Mia Wasikowska is an actress. Alice is her character.

13 Create a movie timetable.

- Choose a movie you like.
- Indicate the cast and the genre of the movie.
- Write a synopsis about the movie.
- Choose the days of the week and the times of the sessions.
- Include a photo or drawing of the movie.

People who care

Good manners

14 Read, stick and then circle or cross out.

Tangente Design/ID/BR

GOOD MANNERS IN THE MOVIE THEATER

When you go to the movies, you want to relax and enjoy the film, but unfortunately some people don't respect others. In libraries, you mustn't talk. In movie theaters, there are clear rules as well and it's important to know them before you go in.

Don't disturb others when you sit.

Switch off your cell phone.

Do not go in late.

Keep cups, cans and boxes with you. Put them in recycling bins after the movies.

Don't have conversations with friends during the movie.

Following these few simple rules will give you and the other people a chance to enjoy the film that you paid to see.

Based on Teen Ink. Why you Should Behave in the Movie Theaters. Available at https://www.teenink.com/opinion/movies_music_tv/article/157679/Why-You-Should-Behave-in-the-Movie-Theaters. Accessed on May 18, 2021.

15 Discuss with your classmates and teacher.

a. What's the most important rule in your opinion?

b. What else do you think it is important when you go to public places? Think about:

- Waiting in line.
- Priority service lines.
- Priority seats.
- Being on time.
- etc.

16 Follow the instructions to finish the movie.

THE MOVIE GAMES

START
Choose "We have to **buy**/**see** the tickets now."
Choose "They like dramas, **and**/**but** they don't like musicals."
Complete "My favorite type of movie is adv■■■■■e."
Choose "We need to **check**/**turn off** the time."
GO FORWARD 1 SPACE
Choose "They like animations **and**/**but** they like action movies."
Complete "I love c■■■■y!"
MISS A TURN
WHAT'S THAT THE MOVIE
3:27 PM
What time does it start?
Mime a movie character
Mime a scene of an action movie
Mime a superhero
GO FORWARD 1 SPACE
TARZAN
11:15 AM
What time does it start?
Mime a princess
GO BACK 2 SPACES
THE END

Workbook
Go to page **118**.

UNIT 4 Having Fun

1 (21) Look, listen and act out.

1
←MIA
Hey Noah. What are you doing?
I'M PLAYING A GAME AND CHATTING ONLINE WITH LUCAS. HE'S SPENDING THE WEEKEND WITH HIS FAMILY AT HIS UNCLE'S FARM. AND YOU?
LUCAS
Just a second Lucas, I'm talking to Mia.

I'M HANGING OUT WITH MY MOM AND THE GIRLS AT THE PARK. ISABELLA AND CHARLOTTE ARE TAKING PICTURES NOW. ANN IS READING COMICS. I'M AT THE PARK NEAR YOUR PLACE. COME DOWN HERE! WE COULD ALL PLAY VOLLEYBALL!
Rafael Rodriz/ID/BR
MOM, CAN I GO MEET THE GIRLS AT THE PARK?
AFTER YOU FINISH YOUR HOMEWORK... BUT... ...ARE YOU PLAYING GAMES, NOAH?
WATER
SORRY, MOM. I'M FINISHING THIS STAGE.
NO, YOU ARE NOT. YOU'RE FINISHING YOUR HOMEWORK NOW, OR YOU ARE IN TROUBLE.
WATER

Language corner

2 Look and stick. Then check the items you like.

FREE TIME ACTIVITIES

Philippe Lissac/Getty Images
MBI/iStock/Getty Images
Rido/Shutterstock.com/ID/BR
Nevada31/Shutterstock.com/ID/BR
Poznyakov/Shutterstock.com/ID/BR
OJO_Images/iStock/Getty Images
Pio3/Shutterstock.com/ID/BR
Mediaphotos/iStock/Getty Images
Franckreporter/iStock/Getty Images

3 Write true sentences about you. Then talk to a classmate.

read	watch	play	listen to	jump	hang out with
chat with	create	paint	take	color	dance

I read comics. / I don't read comics.

4 22 Listen and complete. Then circle Mohammed's free time activities.

Mohammed Yahia

My name is Mohammed Yahia. I am 12 years old. I live with my parents, brothers and sisters near Kabul, in Afghanistan.

This is my routine.

_______________ a.m. – I wake up.

_______________ a.m. – I have breakfast.

_______________ a.m. – I say a prayer. I am Muslim. Then I do some homework.

_______________ a.m. – I usually play soccer with my brother and friends.

_______________ p.m. – I say another prayer at noon.

_______________ p.m. – I have lunch with my family.

_______________ p.m. – It takes me 25 minutes to get to school by bike.

_______________ p.m. – I ride home from school on my bike.

_______________ p.m. – I eat dinner. Then I do more homework and, if there's time, I watch TV.

_______________ p.m. – I go to bed. Good night!

5 Read and complete.

Language Summary	
Mohammed **wakes up** at 7 a.m. **every day**.	It's 7 a.m. Mohammed **is waking up now**.

a. It's eight in the morning. What's Mohammed doing now?

He's having _______________________________.

b. It's nine fifteen in the morning. What's Mohammed doing now?

He's playing _______________________________.

c. It's eight thirty in the evening. What's Mohammed doing now?

He's _______________________________.

6 Look, read and complete.

Language Summary

Image Source Trading Ltd/ Shutterstock.com/ID/BR

Is he dancing?
No, he isn't. He's listening to music.

Jan-Schn/iStock/Getty Images

Is she taking photos?

Yes, ______________ is.

Isitsharp/iStock/Getty Images

Are they playing volleyball?

No, ______________ aren't.

They're ______________ soccer.

Catherine Yeu/iStock/Getty Images

Are you playing video game?

Yes, we are.

PeopleImages/iStock/ Getty Images

A ______________ they jumping ______________?

Yes, ______________.

Jacob Ammentorp/iStock/ Getty Images

B ______________? (draw)

No, ______________

a mandala. (color)

Africa Studio/ Shutterstock.com/ID/BR

C ______________ video game? (play)

No, ______________

a movie. (watch)

7 Mime an action. Ask and answer.

ARE YOU LOOKING AT PHOTOS?
NO, I'M NOT.
ARE YOU READING A BOOK?
YES, I AM.

Werllen Holanda/ID/BR

Sounds like fun

Conteúdo na versão digital

8 (23) Read, listen and say.

doing listen mom

9 (24) Listen and say. Then match the words to the pictures.

- sing**ing** ☐
- ru**n** ☐
- ga**me** ☐
- hang**ing** ☐
- liste**n** ☐
- albu**m** ☐
- ofte**n** ☐

A
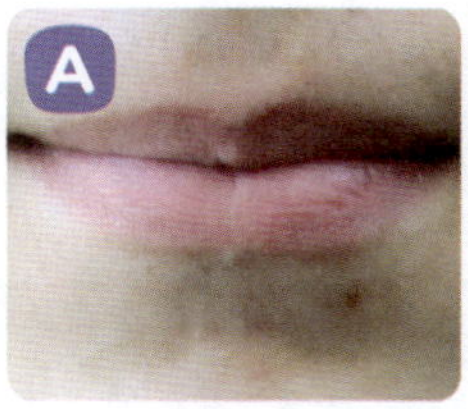
Neuza Faccin/ID/BR

B
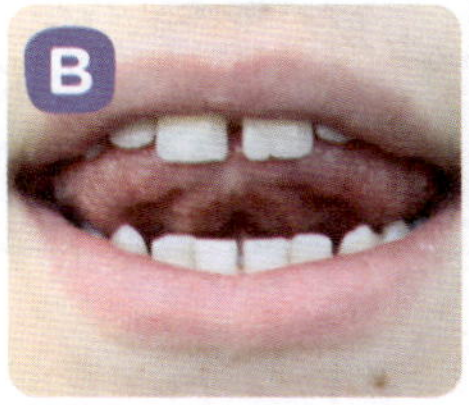
HNfotos/ID/BR

C
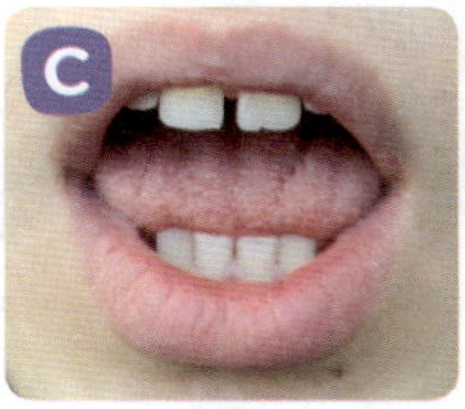
Neuza Faccin/ID/BR

- proble**m** ☐
- read**ing** ☐
- onli**ne** ☐
- far**m** ☐
- swi**m** ☐
- play**ing** ☐
- trai**n** ☐

10 (25) Listen and circle the words people are saying.

some	or	sun
team	or	teen
game	or	gang

hang	or	ham
swing	or	swim
come in	or	coming

11 (26) Read, listen and say.

Ann is running, Adam is swimming, Sheng is singing.

Ahturner/iStock/Getty Images

Karelnoppe/iStock/Getty Images

Sunabesyou/iStock/Getty Images

Time for text

12 Look at the text and check the correct alternative.

The text below is:

- ☐ an informative poster.
- ☐ a timetable.
- ☐ a comic strip.

Sherman's lagoon

HELLO, SHERMAN.
HELLO, MARLEY.
NICE DAY, HUH?
SURE IS.
WHAT ARE YOU DOING?
GETTING A SELFIE OF ME HAVING A NICE DAY.
CLICK
THAT CORAL IS BEAUTIFUL, ISN'T IT?
I GUESS SO.
I NEED A SHOT OF ME WITH THE CORAL.
CLICK
OOH, A SEA HORSE. GOTTA HAVE A PICTURE OF ME WITH A SEA HORSE.
CLICK
LET'S GET ONE OF YOU AND ME.
WHEN DO YOU HAVE TIME TO LOOK AT ALL THESE PICTURES OF YOURSELF?

13 Read the text and match the question to the correct answer.

a. What's Marley doing?	Yes, he is.
b. Is he having a nice day?	Yes, he does.
c. Does Sherman think Marley takes too many photos?	He's taking selfies.

14 Discuss with your classmates and teacher.

a. Do you like taking photos? And selfies?

b. Do you know someone who takes too many photos or selfies?

TIP!

picture = photo **selfie** = photo that you take of yourself.

15 Read and circle the correct word to complete the sentence.

The word "click" in the text represents a **sound/song/letter**.

16 Create a comic strip.

- Look and read some comic strips.
- Create a comic story. Who are the characters? What's happening?
- Decide what words and images you want to use in your comic strip. Can these words represent a sound? If so, which one?
- Write and draw your comic strip.
- Show your comic strip to the class.

People who care

Conteúdo na versão digital

Values

Time with yourself and time with others

17 Look and circle.

In your opinion, which kids are having a good time?

Antoniodiaz/Shutterstock.com/ID/BR

Wavebreakmedia/Shutterstock.com/ID/BR

Littlekidmoment/Shutterstock.com/ID/BR

Daisy Daisy/Shutterstock.com/ID/BR

18 Read and discuss with your classmates and teacher.

> Many experts believe that having free time is one of the most important ways for us to learn, grow, and develop the skills we need to succeed.

Based on Very Well Family. Teaching Your Kids Time Management. Available at https://www.verywellfamily.com/how-to-teach-your-kids-time-management-skills-4126588. Accessed on May 18, 2021.

a. Do you think free time activities are important?

b. What's your favorite free time activity?

c. What do you do to have fun?

d. Is it important to have fun alone? What about with friends?

e. Review this unit and give examples of activities you do alone or with your friends and family.

Games and challenges

19 Look and complete. Then solve the crossword.

1 
MBI/iStock/Getty Images

She's ______________ rope.

2 He's ______________ comics.

Phil's Mommy/ Shutterstock.com/ID/BR

3 
Omgimages/iStock/ Getty Images

She's ______________ out with friends.

SerrNovik/iStock/ Getty Images

4 They're ______________ volleyball.

5 He's ______________ .

Danijela Pavlovic Markov/iStock/Getty Images

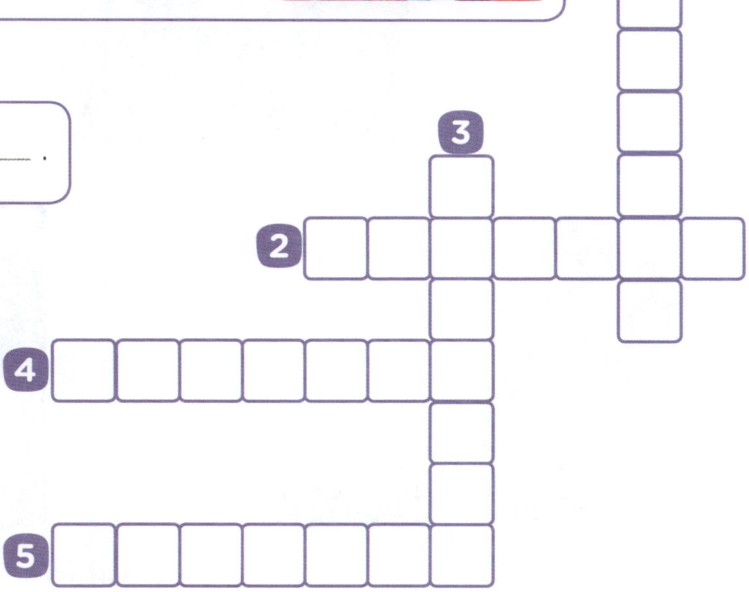
1
2
3
4
5

20 Create a similar crossword in your notebook. Use the words below.

watching taking
creating riding coloring

Workbook
Go to page **120**.

Let's read images!

Leisure and colors

1 Observe the pictures and choose the appropriate option.

A
Fotoksa/iStock/Getty Images

B
IvanMel/Shutterstock.com/ID/BR

C
SolStock/iStock/Getty Images

D
New Africa/Shutterstock.com/ID/BR

E
Jacob Lund/Shutterstock.com/ID/BR

- What do these pictures have in common?

☐ People are spending their free time.

☐ People are exercising.

☐ People are in difficult situations.

2 Now answer these questions.

a. In which picture(s) can you clearly see the place where the person is?

b. In which picture(s) is the activity more important than the person?

c. Do you think the girl in picture D is happy? Explain.

3 Look at the pictures again and answer: What pictures present...

...more vibrant colors?

...serious colors?

...neutral colors?

Follow-up

1 Read and complete the crossword puzzle.

DOWNLOAD

Rawpixel.com/Shutterstock.com/ID/BR

Iakobchuk Viacheslav/Shutterstock.com/ID/BR

Rawpixel.com/Shutterstock.com/ID/BR

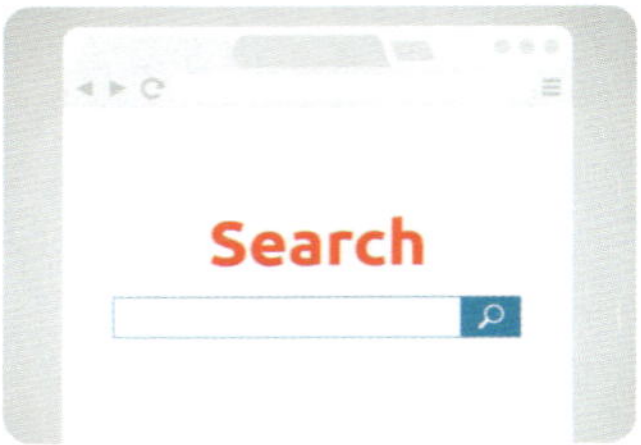
Search

Enraged/Shutterstock.com/ID/BR

Allensima/iStock/Getty Images

Syda Productions/Shutterstock.com/ID/BR

Down ↓

1. The ______________ connection is slow.
4. My dad ______________ on the computer all day long.
5. I love to ______________ with my friends on the tablet.

Across →

2. My sister has to ______________ an e-mail to the school.
3. My older brother loves to ______________ on his laptop.
6. You can ______________ on the Internet to find the information you need.

How many 😊? ☐

2 Solve the riddles, complete and match to the pictures.

A It's small.
It's a mammal.
It makes holes in the ground.
It's ______________________.

B It's big.
It's a rodent mammal.
It lives in groups near rivers and lakes.
It's ______________________.

C It's big.
It's a cat.
It usually has spots on its body.
It's ______________________.

D It's a bird.
It's colorful and noisy.
It can mimic the human voice.
It's ______________________.

E It's a mammal.
It's slow.
It lives in trees.
It's ______________________.

Nacho Such/Shutterstock.com/ID/BR

Martha Marks/Shutterstock.com/ID/BR

Brendan van Son/Shutterstock.com/ID/BR

Christian Vinces/Shutterstock.com/ID/BR

Reto Buhler/Shutterstock.com/ID/BR

How many ?

3 **27** Read, listen and complete.

SCHOOL MOVIE WEEK

Designed by macrovector/ Freepik

Toy Story 4

TOY STORY 4
JUNE 21

Walt Disney Pictures/Pixar Animation Studios/ID/BR

Day: ____________

Time: ____________

animation, comedy, drama

This time, the story revolves around Forky, a toy that Bonnie made and who does not understand his importance in her life. Woody, one more time, goes to his rescue. Action and emotion altogether.

Cinderella

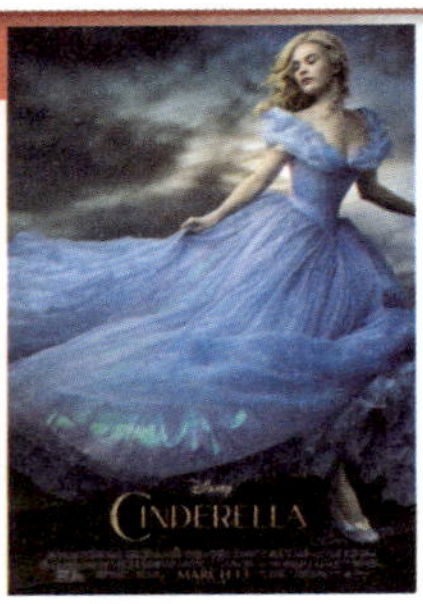
CINDERELLA

Walt Disney Pictures/ID/BR

Day: ____________

Time: ____________

drama, fantasy

When her father dies, young Ella goes to live with her cruel stepmother and her stepsisters. Ella's fortunes begin to change after she meets a charming stranger.

Wall-E

Disney·PIXAR
WALL·E

Pixar Animation Studios/ID/BR

Day: ____________

Time: ____________

animation, adventure

In the distant future, a small waste collecting robot embarks on a space journey that will decide the future of human beings.

Enola Holmes

ENOLA HOLMES
NETFLIX

Legendary Pictures/Netflix/ID/BR

Day: ____________

Time: ____________

action, drama

Enola, a teenager, and Sherlock's sister, tries to find her mother and in doing so, she manages to fool her brother.

Johnny English Strikes Again

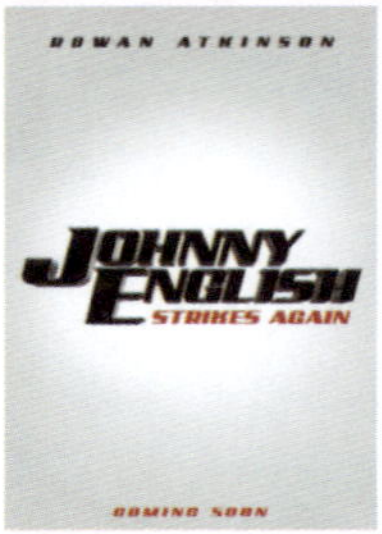
ROWAN ATKINSON
JOHNNY ENGLISH
STRIKES AGAIN
COMING SOON

StudioCanal/Universal Pictures/ID/BR

Day: ____________

Time: ____________

comedy, action

A hacker makes public the information about all secret agents in Britain. The only person who can catch him is someone who knows nothing of technology, and that's Johnny.

Based on IMDb. *Toy Story 4*. Available at https://www.imdb.com/title/tt1979376/?ref_=fn_al_tt_1. *Cinderella*. Available at https://www.imdb.com/title/tt1661199/?ref_=nv_sr_srsg_0. *Wall-E*. Available at https://www.imdb.com/title/tt0910970/?ref_=nv_sr_srsg_0. *Enola Holmes*. Available at https://www.imdb.com/title/tt7846844/?ref_=fn_al_tt_1. *Johnny English Strikes Again*. Available at https://www.imdb.com/title/tt6921996/?ref_=fn_al_tt_1. Accessed on May 19, 2021.

How many 😊? ____

4 Look at the picture and write what Hannah **is** and **isn't** doing now. Use these words.

listen to music | paint | play online games | read comics | take photos

50
100
BONUS

Raitan Ohi/ID/BR

a. ______________________________________.

b. ______________________________________.

c. ______________________________________.

d. ______________________________________.

e. ______________________________________.

How many ☺? ☐

Karaoke
Go to page **112.**

GENERAL SELF-ASSESSMENT - UNITS 1-4

I know the name of some activities I do on the Internet and I know how to identify the parts of a search engine website.	☐	☐	☐
I know how to describe some animals and how to use the adverbs of frequency.	☐	☐	☐
I know how to identify the genre of a movie and read a timetable about movie sessions.	☐	☐	☐
I know the name of some fun activities and how to say what people are doing at the moment.	☐	☐	☐

Illustrations: Alexandre Matos/ID/BR

UNIT 5

Sounds of Music

1 (28) Look, read and listen.

WOW! LOOK... DRAGONFLY... THIS FRIDAY AFTERNOON AT SCHOOL. LET'S GO!
SURE! WHAT DO THEY PLAY? HIP-HOP?
YEP.
DRAGONFLY
at 4pm
Green Village School
SALE
DRAGONFLY
THIS ISN'T HIP-HOP. IT'S ROCK!
YEAH! BUT IT'S GOOD, RIGHT?

HI, GUYS. I'M CAROL AND THIS IS MY FRIEND MISSY. WE LOVED THE SHOW!
THANKS! LET ME INTRODUCE YOU TO THE BAND. I'M CHRIS, I SING AND PLAY THE ELECTRIC GUITAR...
THIS IS TROY, HE PLAYS THE KEYBOARDS. LUCY PLAYS THE BASS, AND KATHY CAN PLAY MANY INSTRUMENTS, BUT IN OUR BAND SHE PLAYS THE DRUMS.
CLASS
I LOVE THE DRUMS, BUT I CAN'T PLAY IT.
I CAN TEACH YOU!
REALLY?! COOL!

Mauro Souza/ID/BR

2 Complete the poster with the correct day of the week.

Language corner

Conteúdo na versão digital

3 (29) Listen and number. Then check the items you like.

FernandoPodolski/iStock/Getty Images

tambourine

Wanida_Sri/Shutterstock.com/ID/BR

piano

Monainshanghai/iStock/Getty Images

guitar

Imgorthand/iStock/Getty Images

harmonica

Artem_Furman/iStock/Getty Images

violin

Meinzahn/iStock/Getty Images

saxophone

AnnettVauteck/iStock/Getty Images

flute

Jupiterimages/Getty Images

cello

Be Good/Shutterstock.com/ID/BR

bass

Studio Gord Horne/iStock/Getty Images

electric guitar

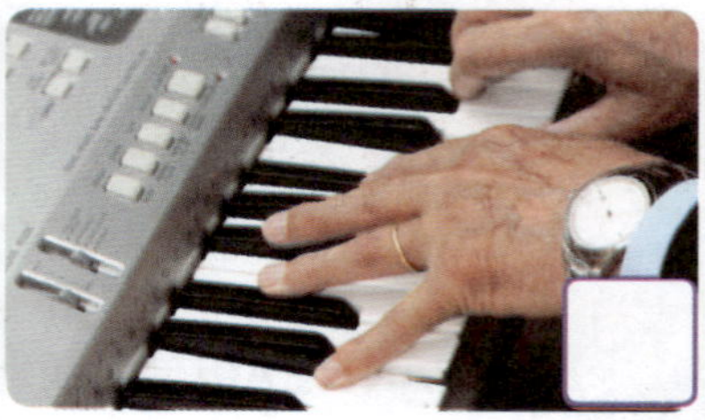
Claudio.arnese/iStock/Getty Images

keyboards

Mr_Twister/iStock/Getty Images

drums

4 Listen to track 29 again and check the correct answer.

What classes are they offering now?
maglyvi/vectorstock.com/ID/BR

- [ ] singing
- [ ] triangle
- [ ] castanets

5 Look, read and complete with the correct information.

Language Summary

I/You/He/She/It/We/You/They	**can play** the piano.
	can't sing.

Illustrations: Mauro Souza/ID/BR

a. Troy ______________ play the keyboards.

b. Lucy ______________ the bass.

c. Kathy ______________ many instruments.

d. Chris ______________ and ______________ the electric guitar.

e. Missy ______________ play the drums, but she wants to learn how to play them.

DRAGONFLY

f. Dragonfly ______________ play very well!

6 Read the dialogues. Then talk to your classmates.

I CAN PLAY THE PIANO. AND YOU? CAN YOU PLAY THE PIANO?
NO, I CAN'T. BUT I CAN PLAY THE DRUMS.

Lisa F. Young/Shutterstock.com/ID/BR

CAN YOU PLAY SOCCER?
NO, I CAN'T. BUT I CAN PLAY HANDBALL VERY WELL.

Rob Hainer/Shutterstock.com/ID/BR

7 (30) Listen and check. Then ask and answer.

What type of music do you like?

a. ☐ classical	b. ☐ pop	c. ☐ rock	d. ☐ *samba*
e. ☐ rap	f. ☐ country	g. ☐ jazz	h. ☐ reggae
i. ☐ *forró*	j. ☐ *axé*	k. ☐ *frevo*	l. ☐ MPB

8 Read the dialogues. Then talk to your classmates.

Samba has its origins in African culture. When Africans arrived in Brazil as slaves, between the 16th and 19th centuries, they brought their customs, traditions and cultures, especially dance and music. Today samba is one of the most famous music and dance styles in Brazil.

Sergio Pedreira/Pulsar Imagens

Mike Monahan/Shutterstock.com/ID/BR

Based on Brazil. Brazil Dance. Available at https://www.brazil.org.za/brazil-dance.html. Accessed on May 18, 2021.

a. Which kind of music from activity 7 is typical in Brazil?

b. Do you know any other music styles influenced by African cultures?

c. Research some Brazilian music styles and share the information with your class.

TIP!

slave = a person who is forced to work very hard in bad conditions and without pay

Conteúdo na versão digital

Sounds like fun

9 (31) Listen and complete the information about music notes.

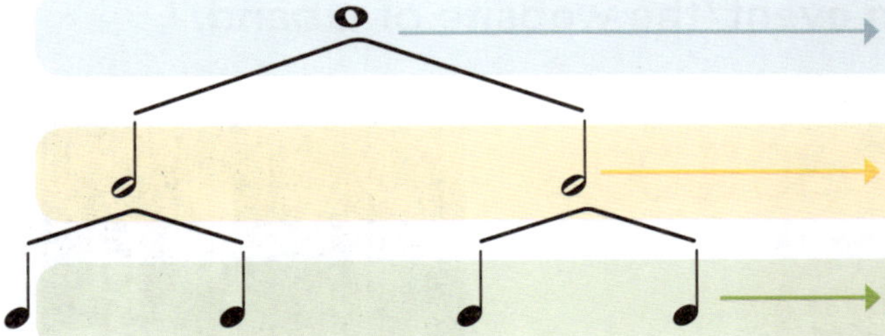

whole note (1) has ______ beats.

half note ($\frac{1}{2}$) has ______ beats.

quarter note ($\frac{1}{4}$) has ______ beat.

10 (32) Read, listen and say.

SAXophone | piAno | guiTAR

11 (33) Listen and circle the strong part of the words in bold.

a. Can you play a musical **in·stru·ment**?

b. I can't play the **key·boards**.

c. I have a beautiful **vi·o·lin**.

d. Do you like the **har·mon·i·ca**?

12 (34) Read, listen and say.

I Can Hear Music

pimonova/vectorstock.com/ID/BR

I can hear music
I can hear music
The sound of the city
baby seems to disappear
I can hear music
Sweet sweet music

Oneinchpunch/Shutterstock.com/ID/BR

Jeff Barry; Ellie Greenwich; Philip Spector. Universal: Songs of PolyGram Int., Inc. *I Can Hear Music*. Available at https://www.songfacts.com/lyrics/the-beach-boys/i-can-hear-music. Accessed on June 16, 2021.

Time for text

13 Look at the text and circle the correct information to complete the sentence.

This text is **a poster inviting to an event/the website of a band**.

ANNUAL PRIMARY SCHOOL
BANDS CONCERT
Little Rock School is proud to present the
40th Annual Primary School Bands Concert
Day Saturday
Date Nov. 26th
Time 3 p.m.
The concert is an amazing opportunity to hear some new bands and musicians. The concert is the result of rehearsals of our students and teachers. See the musical stars of the future perform at this great event!
BANDS PERFORMING:
BLUE LIGHTNING
PURPLE CLOUD
THE BLUEBERRIES
ANN AND THE PUPPETS
Tickets at the Administrative Office

Mike Monahan/Shutterstock.com/ID/BR fet/Shutterstock.com/ID/BR

Terry Vine/Getty Images

14 Read the text and complete.

a. Name of the event: ______________________

b. Day of the week and date of the event: ______________________

c. Time of the event: ______________________

d. Place of the event: ______________________

e. Number of bands performing: ______________________

15 Read the text again and match.

a. concert
b. amazing
c. musicians
d. rehearsal

☐ great
☐ people who play musical instruments and/or sing
☐ a practice of a play or concert
☐ musical show

16 Create an invitation poster for a musical event in your school.

- Complete the chart with the information about the event.

Name of your school	1.
Day of the week and date	2.
Time	3.
City	4.
Number of bands performing	5.

- Read and complete this text with the information from the chart.

(1) ______________________________'s
First Young Musicians Concert

(1) ______________________ is proud to present its First Young Musicians Concert. The concert is **an amazing/ an excellent** opportunity to hear songs played by bands of students. The concert is on (2) ______________________, at (3) ______________________, in (4) ______________________. Come and have fun listening to (5) ______________________ **amazing/great** bands!

Tickets: One kilo of non-perishable food

ID/BR

- Create your own poster in a separate piece of paper. Include photos or drawings.

Values

Respecting music diversity

17 Read, unscramble and stick the correct photo.

Hi, I'm Pedro. My favorite type of music is **msaab**. This is my mom, Bianca, and her favorite kind of music is **crko**. My brother, Lucas, is only 9 years old and he loves **sclaasicl** music. So you can imagine that in our house we listen to many different music styles!

Pedro

Bianca

Lucas

18 Read and match. Then discuss with your classmates and teacher.

a. Diversity means that there are lots of different kinds of things.

b. Everyone can learn more about other cultures, and everyone can share and enjoy the differences.

c. We can see diversity in people's bodies, languages, religion, beliefs, art and, of course, music!

☐ What is great about diversity?

☐ Where can we see diversity?

☐ What is diversity?

Based on Kids Konnect. *How to Teach Your Children About Diversity & Inclusion – Inside and Outside of the Classroom*. Available at https://kidskonnect.com/articles/how-to-teach-your-children-about-diversity-inclusion-inside-and-outside-of-the-classroom/. Accessed on May 18, 2021.

- What kind of music do the members of your family like?
- Is it important to respect musical diversity? Why?
- What about other differences: languages, religion, beliefs, art, etc.?

Games and challenges

19 35 Listen and number the instruments.

Guess the instrument

Adrian Turner/Alamy/Fotoarena

mbira

Joe Potato Photo/iStock/Getty Images

banjo

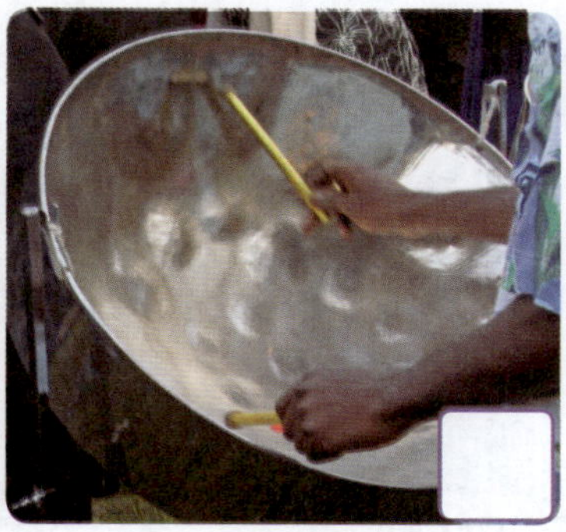
Mark Goddard/iStock/Getty Images

steel drums

Don Emmert/AFP

cajón

Herbert Harmond/iStock/Getty Images

nyckelharpa

Sebastien Bozon/AFP

theremin

Workbook
Go to page **122**.

Design by Freepik

UNIT

6 I'm not Feeling Well

1 36 Look, listen and read. Then act out.

EVERYBODY READY TO PLAY?
YEAH!
LET'S WIN THE GAME!
KEN, ARE YOU ALL RIGHT?
NOT REALLY. I'M NOT FEELING WELL.
WHAT'S THE MATTER?
I HAVE A SORE THROAT AND A HEADACHE. SORRY, BUT I CAN'T PLAY.
COUGH
COUGH
COUGH

Rafael Rodriz/ID/BR
HEY! COVER YOUR MOUTH WITH YOUR ARM.
SORRY.
AND IF YOU USE YOUR HANDS, YOU HAVE TO WASH THEM!
YOU'RE RIGHT.
ANYWAY... I SEE YOU HAVE A COUGH AND A RUNNY NOSE. DO YOU HAVE A FEVER?
I DON'T THINK SO. BUT I'M DIZZY TOO.
MAYBE YOU HAVE A COLD OR THE FLU OR SOMETHING.
I'M CALLING MY SISTER.
KEN GOES TO THE DOCTOR WITH HIS OLDER SISTER.
IT'S NOTHING SERIOUS, BOY. IT'S JUST A COLD. YOU'LL BE OK IN FOUR OR FIVE DAYS.
HERE'S THE PRESCRIPTION, MS. COVERDALE.
I'LL TAKE CARE OF YOU, BUDDY!

Language corner

2 Read and look. Then match the sentences to the photos.

a. Oh, I have a terrible **headache**.

b. He has a **cough**. He needs to see a doctor.

c. I have to see a dentist. I have a **toothache**.

d. I'm feeling bad! I have a **stomachache**.

e. My ears! I have an **earache**.

f. You have a **runny nose**. Are you OK?

Andresr/iStock/Getty Images

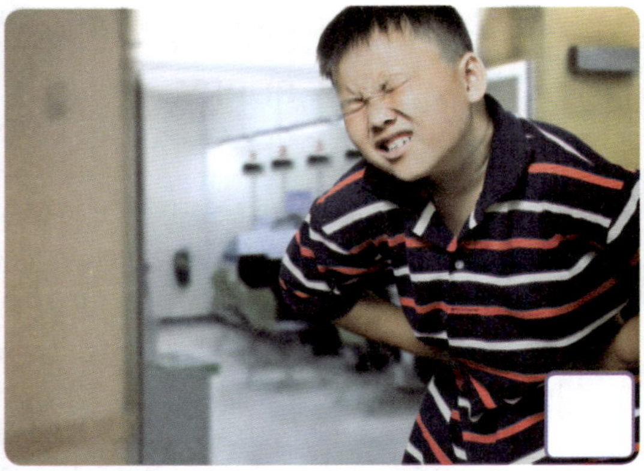

Coward_lion/iStock/Getty Images

Steve Debenport/iStock/Getty Images

Philipimage/Shutterstock.com/ID/BR

G-stockstudio/iStock/Getty Images

Laflor/iStock/Getty Images

3 37 Look and read. Then listen and complete.

Conteúdo na versão digital

Language Summary

I/you/they — **have** — a headache. He/she/it — **has** — a cough.	I — **am** You/we/they — **are** — dizzy. He/She/It — **is**

sore throat | not hungry | fever | nauseous | bruise | sneezing

a.

KatarzynaBialasiewicz/iStock/Getty Images

He's ______________________.

b.

Perkmeup/iStock/Getty Images

She has a ______________________.

c.

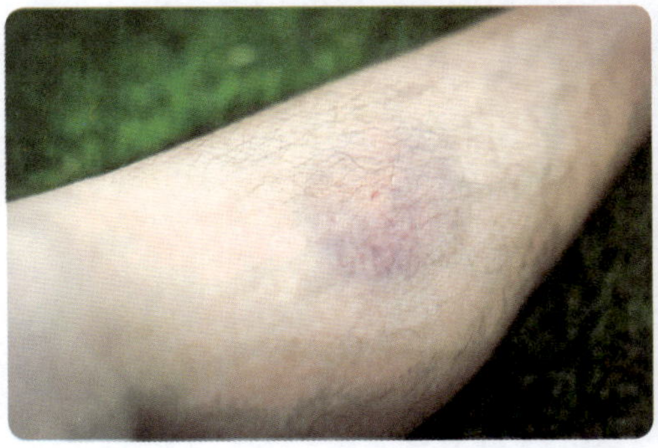

SingjaiStock/Shutterstock.com/ID/BR

He has a ______________________.

d.

DrGrounds/iStock/Getty Images

She's ______________________.

e.

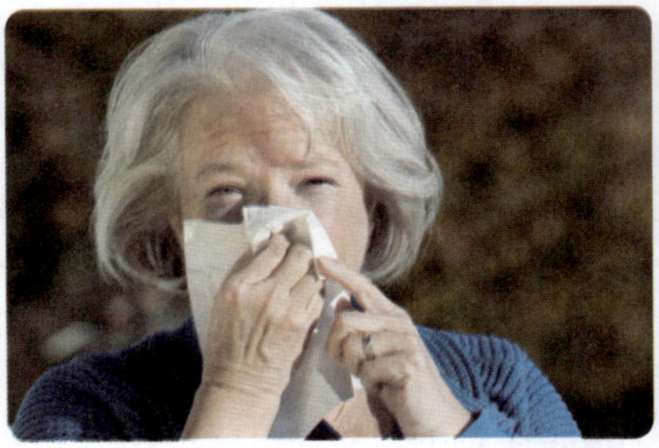

Dora Zett/Shutterstock.com/ID/BR

She's ______________________.

f.

Pathdoc/Shutterstock.com/ID/BR

I'm ______________________.

4 Read the chart and write sentences.

If I have/I'm	I may have
a stomachache, nauseous	food poisoning
a runny nose, a fever, a sore throat, a cough	a cold

Example: If I have a stomachache, I may have food poisoning.

____

____

TIP!

I may have = it's possible that I have

5 Read and complete. Then talk to a classmate.

WHAT'S THE MATTER?
I HAVE ______________./
I'M ______________.
GO SEE THE NURSE/A DOCTOR/ THE TEACHER/SOME ADULT.

Laurence Mouton/PhotoAlto/Getty Images

6 Discuss with your classmates and teacher.

a. Do you sometimes have health problems? Which ones?

b. If you are not well, do you talk to someone? Who?

Sounds like fun

7 (38) Listen and answer. Then talk to your classmates.

What's the difference in sound between these two words?

mou**th** **th**at

8 (39) Listen and repeat. Then write the words in the correct column.

throat this three tooth mother the Math they

/θ/ as in mouth	/ð/ as in that

9 (40) Listen and say this tongue twister.

This Thursday, Theo's mother had a toothache and her face/cheek is sore.

THURSDAY
25

Studio 58/ID/BR

Time for text

10 Read the prescription and follow the instructions below.

- Circle the information about the patient in red.
- Circle the medicine and quantity in blue.
- Circle the doctor's recommendation in green.
- Circle the doctor's signature and identification in black.

Patient's name: Ken Coverdale

Address: 10 Matthew St.

City: Seattle, WA ZIP: 98108

Age: 10 – Guardian: Melissa Coverdale (sister)

℞

- Vitamin C supplement

1 tablet per day for 5 days

Recommendation:

- Drink a lot of water
- Eat well
- Get some rest

Common cold

Refill 0 times

Date: Sept. 5, 2022

Doctor Jane Smith
M.D. D.E.A. AB5623740
Jane Smith

11 Read the prescription again and answer the questions.

a. What is Ken's full name? ______________________.

b. Where does he live? ______________________.

c. How old is he? ______________________.

d. Who is Melissa? ______________________.

e. What problem does Ken have? ______________________.

f. What does the doctor prescribe? How many tablets a day?

______________________.

g. What does the doctor recommend?

______________________.

12 Read the recipe and circle **yes** or **no**.

Juice Recipe for Colds

Our bodies can fight off colds, especially if they have the right nutrients. Juice is an easy and delicious way to get your body vitamins and minerals.

HNfotos/ID/BR

Ingredients

- Apples – 2 large
- Lime – 1/2 fruit
- Strawberries – 3 cups

Directions

Process all ingredients in a juicer, shake or mix and serve.

Based on Hello Glow. *3 Seasonal Superfood Cold-Fighting Juice Recipes*. Available at https://helloglow.co/healthy-juice-recipes-for-colds. Accessed on May 18, 2021.

a. Does our body defend itself from colds? Yes/No

b. Is juice one manner to help our body get vitamins? Yes/No

c. Is the juice above indicated for toothache? Yes/No

13 Read the text again and match the words to their meanings.

juicer	to combine ingredients to form one substance
shake	a machine for extracting juice from fruits and vegetables
mix	to offer food or drink to someone
serve	to make quick movements up and down and side to side

14 Write a juice recipe in your notebook.

- Write a juice recipe in your notebook. Research some fruits, vegetables and other ingredients. Talk to your family and teacher.
- Make a list of the ingredients of your juice.
- Write down the instructions on how to prepare it.
- Show your recipe to your classmates and teacher.

Conteúdo na versão digital

Values

Healthy tips: preventing the flu or a cold

15 Read the text and stick.

LattaPictures/iStock/Getty Images

tangente design/ID/BR

Healthy tips: preventing a cold

How can we prevent getting a cold? Paulo, 10 years old

Hi, Paulo. Your question is very important, especially during the winter, when many people have a cold or the flu. I have some special tips for you and your friends.

- Use separate cups and utensils.
  Using someone's cups, spoons or forks can spread viruses.
- Wash your hands and use hand sanitizer, if possible.
  This is one of the best ways to stop the spread of viruses that may bring you a cold, pneumonia and other problems.
- Cough into your arm.
  Cough or sneeze into the inside of your elbow. This prevents the viruses from spreading.

To keep healthy and prevent having other health problems, remember:

- Clean all containers of stagnant water. This prevents proliferation of mosquitoes and other insects.
- Always brush your teeth after your meals. This prevents tooth cavities.
- Stay home when you have a contagious disease.
- Eat fresh, clean and healthy food.

Spread the word (not viruses!) and be healthy!

16 Discuss with your classmates and teacher.

a. Do you usually follow the instructions mentioned in the text?

b. Are they important? Why?

c. Can you think of other important recommendations for good health?

Games and challenges

17 Find the words to complete the dialogue.

G	T	Y	N	E	A	Y	A	W	G
P	O	M	A	T	T	E	R	A	O
O	R	O	U	S	O	R	E	T	I
C	B	A	S	R	P	D	S	E	T
S	W	F	E	V	E	R	U	R	G
D	A	C	O	M	H	E	A	Y	A
E	T	O	U	F	G	S	Y	P	O
M	P	E	S	B	O	T	O	A	C
Z	E	A	T	Q	A	L	S	D	B
V	W	H	E	A	D	A	C	H	E

GOOD MORNING, MS. GOUVEIA! SO, WHAT'S THE M _ _ _ _ _?

Wavebreak/iStock/Getty Images

I HAVE A SORE THROAT AND A TERRIBLE H _ _ _ _ _ _ _. I'M N _ _ _ _ _ _ _ TOO.

DO YOU HAVE A F _ _ _ _?

YES, IT IS ABOUT 38 DEGREES.

TAKE THIS MEDICINE, DRINK A LOT OF W _ _ _ _, E _ _ WELL AND GET SOME R _ _ _. COME BACK IN FIVE DAYS.

Wavebreak/iStock/Getty Images

SURE! THANK YOU, DOCTOR.

Workbook
Go to page **124**.

People and places

Diverse instruments

1 Read and write the names of the instruments.

DoraDalton/iStock/Getty Images

Ivanfolio/Shutterstock.com/ID/BR

OlegAlbinsky/iStock/Getty Images

Denkou Images/Getty Images

Golero/iStock/Getty Images

Lloyd Pierre/Getty Images

The ***berimbau*** is a percussion instrument with only one string. It is the main instrument used to accompany *capoeira*, a Brazilian martial art.

Based on: Center for World Music. Available at https://centerforworldmusic.org/2015/06/world-music-instruments-the-berimbau. Accessed on April 8, 2021.

The **Mbira** is a folk instrument originally from Africa and traditional in Zimbabwe. Sometimes called a Thumb Piano, it has metal tongues and is played with the thumbs.

Based on: Soniccouture. Available at https://www.soniccouture.com/en/products/26-percussion/g22-array-mbira. Accessed on April 8, 2021.

The **didgeridoo** is a wind instrument made from wood. The first didgeridoos, played by aboriginal peoples in northern Australia, are from 40,000 years ago.

Based on: Didge Project. Available at https://www.didgeproject.com/free-didgeridoo-lessons/what-is-a-didgeridoo. Accessed on April 8, 2021.

The **guitar** probably originated in Spain in the 16th century. First, it had only 4 strings, but the modern guitar has 6 strings.

Based on: *Britannica*. Available at https://www.britannica.com/art/guitar. Accessed on April 8, 2021.

The **bagpipe** is a musical wind instrument with pipes and a bag that is air supplied endlessly. It became very famous in Scotland.

Based on: Cmuse. Available at https://www.cmuse.org/bagpipes. Accessed on April 8, 2021.

Steel drums are percussion instruments originated in Trinidad and Tobago in the 20th century. The drums are played with specific sticks.

Based on: Wikipedia. Available at https://en.wikipedia.org/wiki/Steelpan#Classification. Accessed on April 8, 2021.

2 Write the name of each instrument in the correct country on the map.

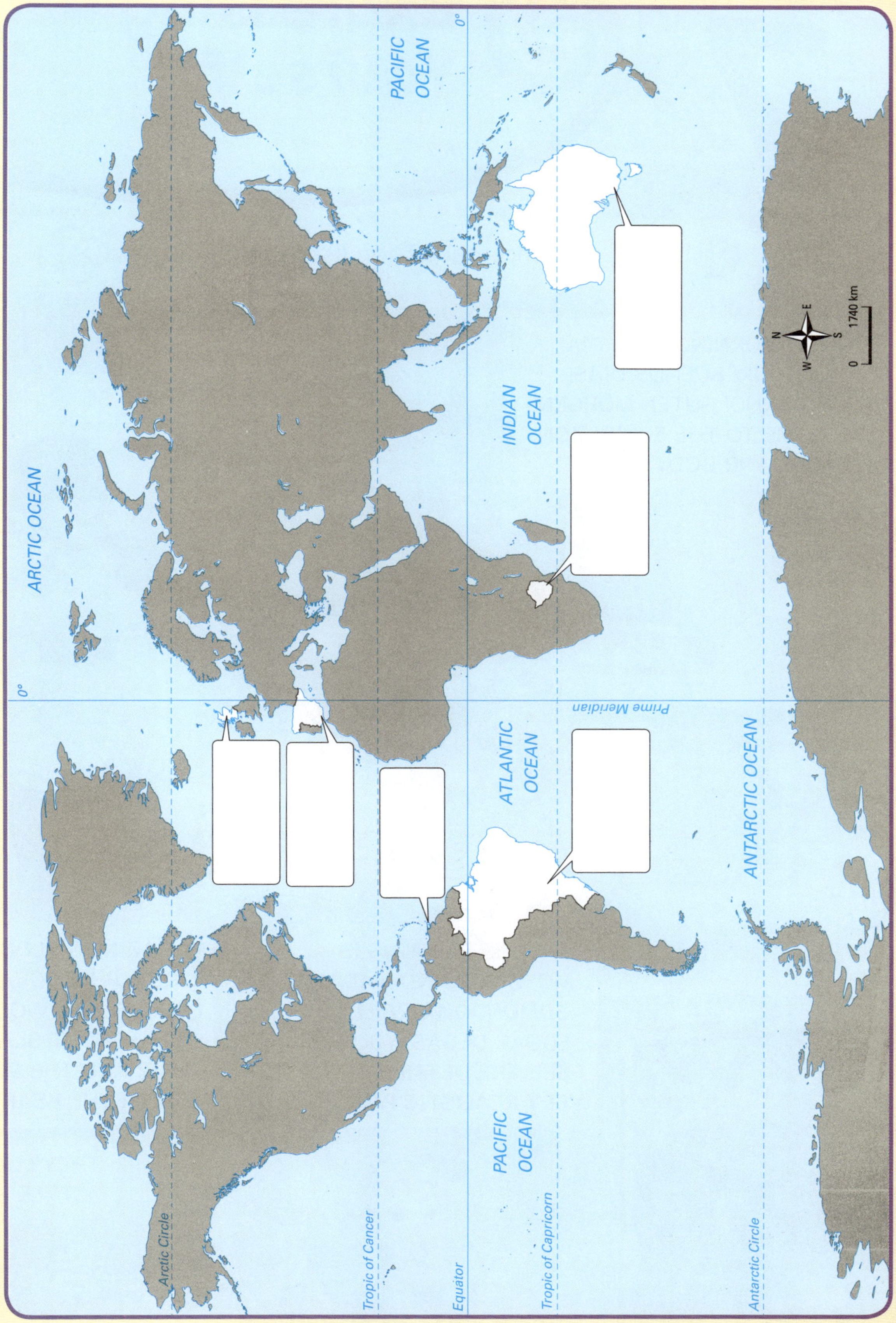
ARCTIC OCEAN
PACIFIC OCEAN
INDIAN OCEAN
ATLANTIC OCEAN
PACIFIC OCEAN
ANTARCTIC OCEAN
Arctic Circle
Tropic of Cancer
Equator
Tropic of Capricorn
Antarctic Circle
Prime Meridian
0°
0°
N
S
E
W
0
1740 km

João Miguel A. Moreira/ID/BR

UNIT 7

Expressing Yourself

1 (41) Look and read. Then listen and act out.

GOOD MORNING! BOM DIA! BONJOUR! BUENOS DIAS! BUONGIORNO! GUTEN MORGEN! WELCOME TO THE EXHIBITION "FACES AND BODY IN ART"!
MERCI!
THANKS!!
WOW, HE CAN SPEAK SO MANY LANGUAGES!
THIS PAINTING IS *MONSIEUR AND MADAME EDMONDO MORBILLI*, BY EDGAR DEGAS. YOU CAN SEE THE DETAILS. IT'S A VERY REALISTIC PAINTING.
AMAZING! IT LOOKS LIKE A PHOTOGRAPH! LOOK AT THE WOMAN WITH SHORT BLACK HAIR AND THE MAN WITH THE BEARD.
THEY LOOK A LITTLE SAD.
Museum of Fine Arts, Boston. Photography: Akg-images/Album/Fotoarena

THIS PAINTING IS BY THE BRAZILIAN ARTIST ALBERTO DA VEIGA GUIGNARD...
YEAH. BUT I THINK THE PAINTING IS BEAUTIFUL...
THIS WOMAN LOOKS SAD TOO.
I REALLY LIKE THIS ONE, BUT IT'S NOT A PAINTING.
YOU'RE RIGHT, IT'S NOT A PAINTING, BUT IT'S ART. IT'S A DRAWING BY LEONARDO DA VINCI. DO YOU KNOW HIM?
YES! HE'S THE PAINTER OF _______________!
THAT'S CORRECT!
NOW WE CONTINUE WITH THE SCULPTURES. THIS IS *ADAM* BY AUGUSTE RODIN.
WOW! HE IS VERY TALL!

Museum Casa Guignard, Ouro Preto/Raquel, Isabel e Helena Lacerda. Photography: Heitor Cavalheiro

Galleria degli Uffizi, Florence. Photography: Bridgeman/Fotoarena

Mauro Souza/ID/BR

Philadelphia Museum of Art, Pennsylvania. Photography: Bridgeman/Fotoarena

2 Write the name of Da Vinci's painting.

Language corner

3 (42) Listen and complete the profiles. Then write your profile.

Spanish French Italian German Mandarin

A

Hogan Imaging/Shutterstock.com/ID/BR

Name: Sophie
Country: France

She can speak ______________ and English.

B

Rido/Shutterstock.com/ID/BR

Name: Pablo
Country: Argentina

He can speak ______________ and English.

C

Brian Smith/iStock/Getty Images

Name: Hans
Country: Germany

He can speak ______________, English and Spanish.

D

Goodluz/Shutterstock.com/ID/BR

Name: Francesca
Country: Italy

She can speak ______________, English and French.

E

Naka-stockphoto/Shutterstock.com/ID/BR

Name: Kejun Pu
Country: China

She can speak ______________, English and Portuguese.

Name: ______________
Country: ______________

I can speak ______________
______________.

4 Ask and answer.

CAN YOU SPEAK SPANISH?

YES, I CAN.

NO, I CAN'T.

5 Read and match the sentences to the images.

a. woman with short black hair

b. man with a beard

c. blond woman

Sterling and Francine Clark Art Institute, Williamstown. Photography: Bridgeman/Fotoarena
Museum of Fine Arts, Boston. Photography: Akg-images/Album/Fotoarena
Museum of Fine Arts, Boston. Photography: Akg-images/Album/Fotoarena

6 Look, read and complete with the words from the box.

Conteúdo na versão digital

black	brown	short	red	blue	green

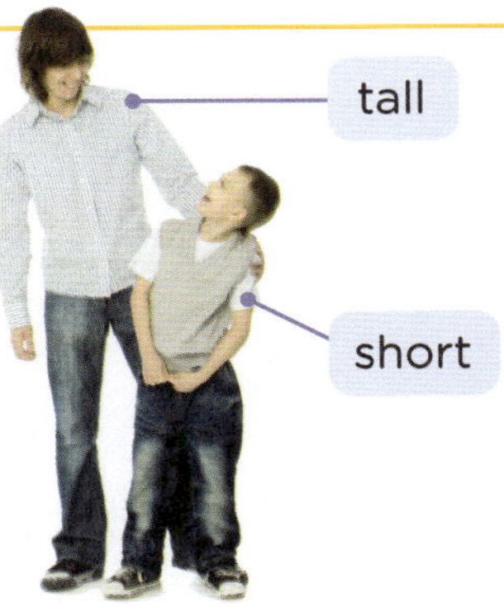
tall
short

Doublephoto Studio/Shutterstock.com/ID/BR

Tatomm/iStock/Getty Images

long ____________ hair

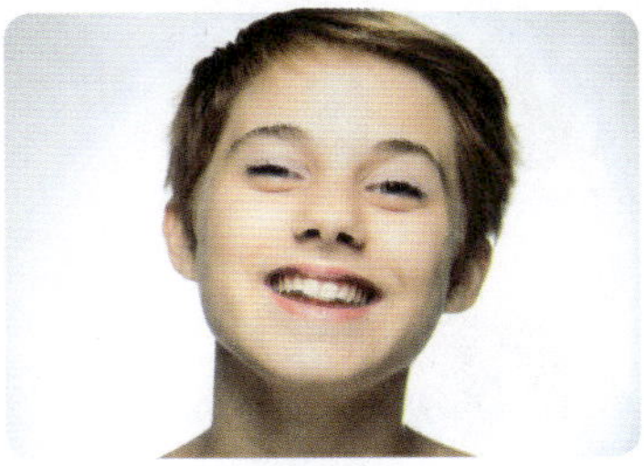

BalicDalibor/iStock/Getty Images

____________ blond hair

William Moss/Shutterstock.com/ID/BR

curly ____________ hair

Mtreasure/iStock/Getty Images

straight ____________ hair

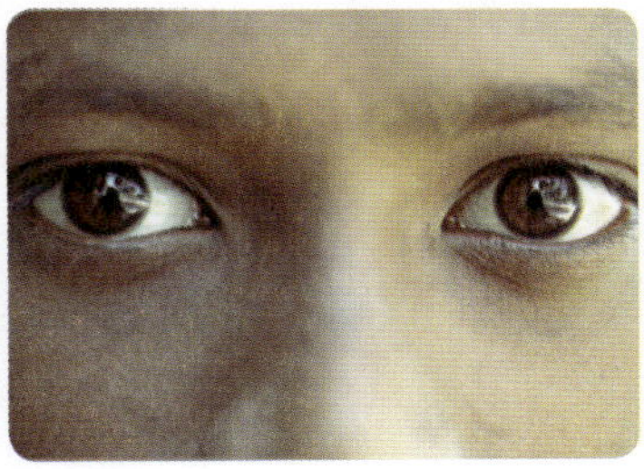

V.s.anandhakrishna/Shutterstock.com/ID/BR

brown eyes

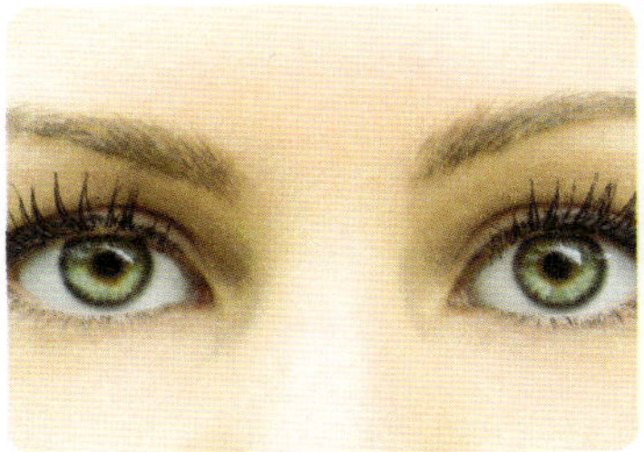

Sruilk/Shutterstock.com/ID/BR

____________ eyes

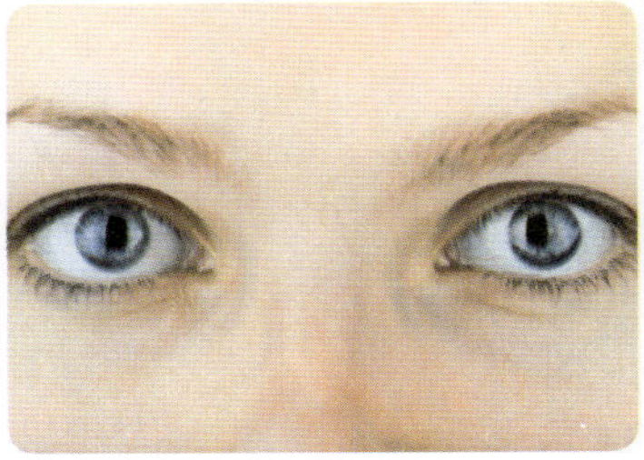

Robnroll/Shutterstock.com/ID/BR

____________ eyes

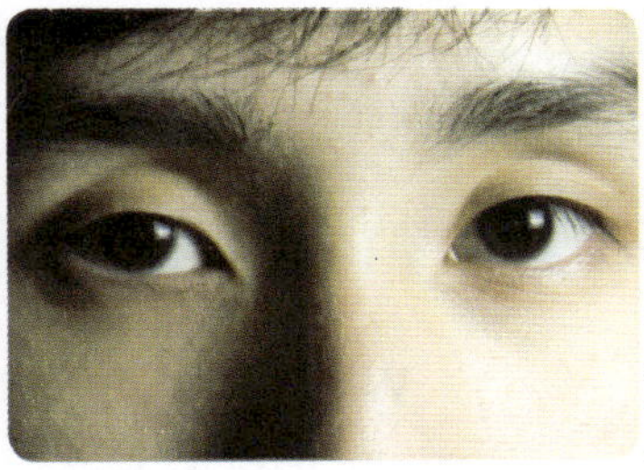

Bangkokhappiness/Shutterstock.com/ID/BR

dark brown eyes

7 Read and answer the questions.

Language Summary

What **do** you look like? What **does** he look like? What **does** she look like?	He **is** She **is** I **am**	tall. short.
	He **has** She **has** I **have**	long/short hair. straight/curly hair. blond/black/brown/red hair. blue/green/brown/dark brown eyes. a beard.

Salez/iStock/Getty Images

A

What does he look like?

He is short and he has long straight black

__________ and dark brown __________.

Samuel Borges Photography/ Shutterstock.com/ID/BR

B

What does she look like?

She is tall and she has __________ curly

brown hair and __________ eyes.

C

What do you look like?

I am __________ and I have __________

__________ hair and.

__________ eyes.

8 Describe someone you know. Ask and answer questions.

WHAT DOES YOUR BEST FRIEND LOOK LIKE?

WELL, SHE IS SHORT, AND SHE HAS LONG CURLY BLACK HAIR AND BROWN EYES.

Sounds like fun

9 (43) Listen and circle the stressed words in the sentences.

a. What does he look like? He is tall.

b. What does she look like? She is short.

c. What do you look like? I am not very tall.

10 (44) Read, listen and say.

He is tall.

He**'s** tall.

She is short.

She**'s** short.

I am not very tall.

I**'m** not very tall.

What does he look like?

What **does he** look like?

What does she look like?

What **does she** look like?

What do you look like?

What **do you** look like?

11 (45) Read and listen. Then look and check.

Vincent (Starry, starry night)

Starry, starry night,
Paint your palette **blue** and **gray**
Look out on a **summer's day**
With eyes that know the darkness in my soul
Starry, starry night
Flaming flowers that brightly blaze
Swirling clouds in violet haze
Reflect in Vincent's eyes of china blue

Don McLean. *Vincent (Starry, starry night)*. Available at https://wordsmusicandstories.wordpress.com/2019/08/01/vincent-starry-starry-night-2-analysis/comment-page-1/. Accessed on June 21, 2021.

Croisy/iStock/Getty Images

Van Gogh Museum, Amsterdam. Photography: ID/BR

Museum of Modern Art, New York. Photography: ID/BR

Minneapolis Institute of Arts, USA. Photography: Minneapolis Institute of Art/The William Hood Dunwoody Fund/Bridgeman Images/Fotoarena

Time for text

12 Read and complete the infoboxes. Then stick.

artist year dimensions location material title

	[sticker]	[sticker]
______	Alberto da Veiga Guignard (1896-1962)	Leonardo da Vinci (1452-1519)
______	*Retrato de Regina Lacerda*	*Mona Lisa (La Gioconda)*
______	1961	1503-1505
______	Oil on canvas	Oil on panel
______	65 cm × 50 cm	77 cm × 53 cm
______	Museu Casa Guignard, Brazil	Musée du Louvre, Paris, France

Based on: MAM. Guignard. A memória plástica do Brasil. Available at https://mam.org.br/wp-content/uploads/2015/12/MAMbx.pdf; *Britannica*. Mona Lisa. Available at https://www.britannica.com/topic/Mona-Lisa-painting. Accessed on May 18, 2021.

13 Read the infoboxes again and answer.

a. Which painting is in France right now?

______.

b. Which painting is smaller (see the dimensions)?

______.

14 Read the text and create an infobox about the painting.

Museum of Contemporary Art, São Paulo. Photography: Romulo Fialdini/Tempo Composto

This self-portrait (when somebody paints himself/herself) painted by the Brazilian painter Alberto da Veiga Guignard (1896-1962) is simply called *Self-Portrait*. It is an oil on wood executed in 1931 and it is 62.2 cm × 50.6 cm. It is currently displayed at the Museum of Contemporary Art, University of São Paulo.

Artist	______
Title	______
Year	______
Material	______
Dimensions	______
Location	______

15 Look at Guignard's painting again and complete.

Conteúdo na versão digital

short Brazil Brazilian straight

Alberto da Veiga Guignard, a famous ______ painter, was born in 1896 in Nova Friburgo, ______. In his *Self-Portrait* he has ______ ______ gray hair.

People who care

Values

Art and language

16 46 Read, listen and sing.

The mosquito

No me moleste mosquito
No me moleste mosquito
No me moleste mosquito
Why don't you go home
No me moleste mosquito
Let me eat my burrito
No me moleste mosquito
Why don't you go home

mstay/iStock/Getty Images

The Doors. Alchemical Music. *No me moleste mosquito*. Available at https://genius.com/The-doors-the-mosquito-lyrics. Accessed on June 21, 2021.

17 Look at the signs, learn and practice.

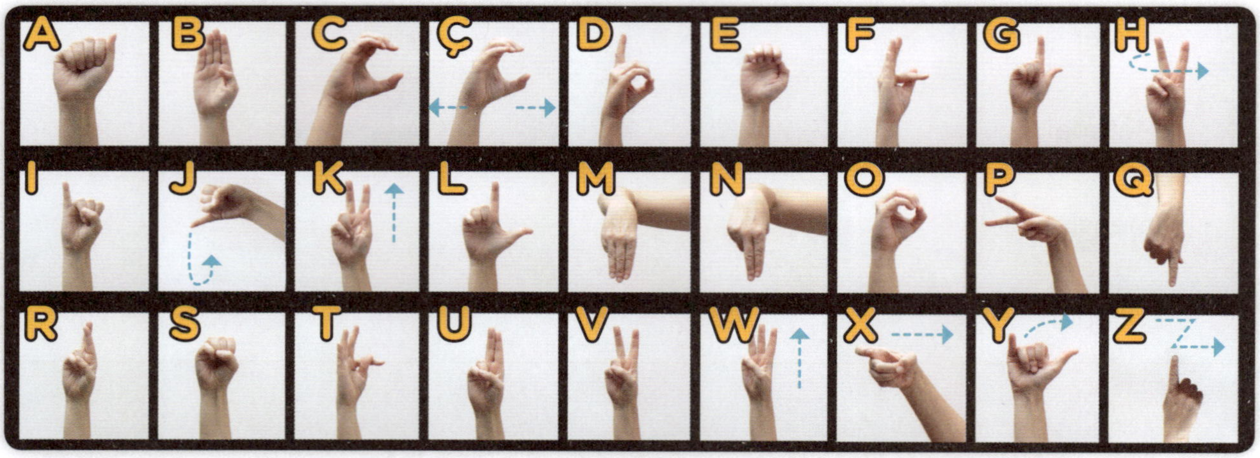
A B C Ç D E F G H
I J K L M N O P Q
R S T U V W X Y Z

Fernando Favoretto/Criar Imagem

18 Discuss with your classmates and teacher.

a. Can we express ourselves only through written and spoken language?

b. Do you think these items are forms of communication? Can we express ourselves through them?

- music
- sculpture
- gesture
- painting
- drawing
- facial expression

Games and challenges

19 Play tic-tac-toe.

Tverdohlib/iStock/Getty Images

He has

Vuk8691/iStock/Getty Images

She has

DRB Images, LLC/iStock/Getty Images

He's

Donna Coleman/iStock/Getty Images

He has

Johnny Greig/iStock/Getty Images

He's

Neustockimages/iStock/Getty Images

She has

EMPPhotography/iStock/Getty Images

He has

McInnich/iStock/Getty Images

She has

Sirikornt/iStock/Getty Images

He has

VvoeVale/iStock/Getty Images

Workbook
Go to page **126**.

UNIT 8

Vacation Time

1 (47) Listen, read and act out.

WHAT DO YOU LIKE DOING ON VACATION, VALENTINA?
I LOVE GOING TO THE BEACH.
ME TOO. AND WHAT DO YOU DO THERE?
I LIKE PLAYING MATKOT, COLLECTING SEASHELLS...
COLLECTING SEASHELLS? THAT'S FOR BABIES!
NO, IT'S NOT! I HAVE A BEAUTIFUL COLLECTION. YOU HAVE TO SEE IT.
ALL RIGHT. I LOVE SWIMMING IN THE SEA.

OH, I DON'T LIKE SWIMMING, BUT I LIKE EATING SEAFOOD.
ON THE BEACH?!
AT HOME OR AT A SEAFOOD RESTAURANT. WE LOVE COOKING SEAFOOD AT HOME TOO. ON THE BEACH WE USUALLY JUST DRINK LOTS OF COCONUT WATER.
MY FAVORITE VACATION ACTIVITY IS GOING TO AMUSEMENT PARKS.
THAT'S FUN, BUT EXPENSIVE...
Rafael Rodriz/ID/BR
I KNOW. BUT WE USUALLY SPEND MOST OF OUR VACATION HERE. I LIKE VISITING MY AUNTS AND UNCLES.
I LOVE SEEING MY FAMILY TOO. BUT THEY LIVE FAR AWAY, SO I ONLY GO THERE ONCE IN A WHILE.

Language corner

2 Look, read and write.

cook go to amusement parks go to the beach play matkot
swim in the sea travel go to the countryside do arts and crafts visit family

PenelopeB/iStock/Getty Images

Fuchs-photography/iStock/Getty Images

Racheal Grazias/Shutterstock.com/ID/BR

Justin Horrocks/iStock/Getty Images

Oneblink-cj/iStock/Getty Images

Susan Chiang/iStock/Getty Images

Cristian M/Shutterstock.com/ID/BR

Ioan Florin Cnejevici/iStock/Getty Images

Andresr/iStock/Getty Images

3 48 Listen and write the initials in the boxes of activity 2. What do they like doing?

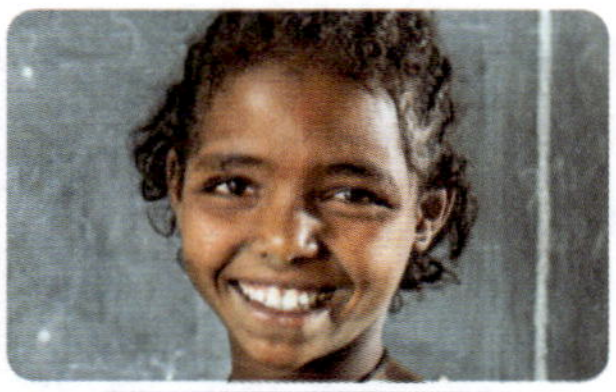

Bartosz Hadyniak/iStock/Getty Images

Laura

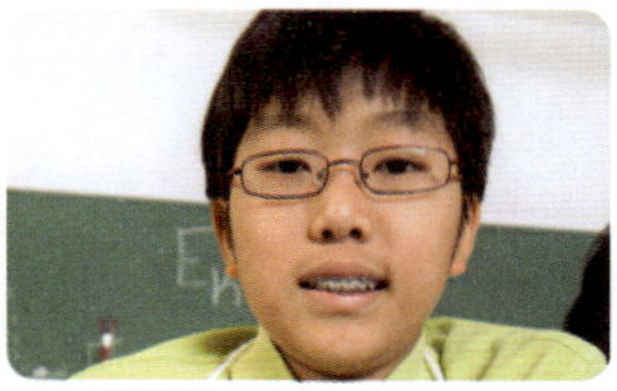

Pamela Moore/iStock/Getty Images

Bruno

Linda Yolanda/iStock/Getty Images

Karen

4 Read and talk to your classmates.

Language Summary			
What **do**	you / they	**like doing** on vacation?	I **love swimming**. We **don't like going to** the beach. They **like going to** amusement parks.
What **does**	he / she	**like doing** on vacation?	He **loves cooking**. She **hates traveling**. He **doesn't like playing** matkot.

5 Choose two free time activities and interview your classmates.

		Count the answers here
Do you like ____________________?	Yes.	____________________ ____________________
	No.	____________________ ____________________
Do you like ____________________?	Yes.	____________________ ____________________
	No.	____________________ ____________________

6 Present your results to the class.

MBI/Shutterstock.com/ID/BR

TWENTY CLASSMATES LIKE SWIMMING IN A POOL AND FIVE CLASSMATES DON'T LIKE IT.

Conteúdo na versão digital

7 (49) Listen and check the food items mentioned.

TOTAL R$	**140,00**
Cash	150,00
Change R$	10,00

spaghetti ☐
Gbh007/iStock/Getty Images

Caesar salad ☐
NightAndDayImages/iStock/Getty Images

grilled chicken ☐
Dr911/iStock/Getty Images

shrimps ☐
Artem Kalashnikov/Shutterstock.com/ID/BR

coconut water ☐
Everydayplus/iStock/Getty Images

mashed potato ☐
Vikif/iStock/Getty Images

French fries ☐
Ajafoto/iStock/Getty Images

fish fillet with vegetables ☐
Kelly Cline/iStock/Getty Images

fruit juices ☐
Anna Kucherova/Shutterstock.com/ID/BR

fruit salad ☐
EasyBuy4u/iStock/Getty Images

ice cream cone ☐
Billyfoto/iStock/Getty Images

FRESH
LEMON
DRINK
soft drink ☐
Oleksiy Mark/iStock/Getty Images

8 Look, read and complete the numbers.

140 ______ one hundred and forty ______

200 ______________________ hundred

355 three ______________________ and fifty-five

480 ______________________ and eighty

529 ______________________ and twenty-nine

601 ______________________ and ______________

799 ______________________ and ninety-nine

800 ______________________

937 ______________________ and ______________

Sounds like fun

9 (50) Listen to these compound words. Then circle and repeat.

ice cream soft drink French fries

Which part of the word has more emphasis?

10 (51) Listen, circle and say. Then stick.

A coconut water

B amusement park

C swimming pool

D popcorn

E seafood

F granola bar

11 Do you know any other compound words in English? Talk to a classmate.

12 (52) Listen and repeat the sentences.

Coconut water, coconut water, coconut water, coconut water...
Soft drink, soft drink, soft drink, soft drink, soft drink, soft drink, soft drink...
Swimming pool, swimming pool, swimming pool, swimming pool, chhhhhhhhh.

Tangente Design/ID/BR

13 Make your own compound words and say them.

Time for text

14 Look at the text and circle the correct information.

The text is a **school website/search engine website/ discussion forum**.

http://www.caloriecount.com/forums/foods/bestfoodawayfromhome

welcome to: forums > food > best food away from home

Best Food Away from Home

Moderator: cult2014on

RedlineVector/iStock/Getty Images

letninja

Sept. 14 at 2:31 p.m.

Hello. I'm going to an amusement park on Saturday with friends. I know they usually have pizza, soft drinks, ice cream, French fries and other junk food. But I want to eat and drink good healthy food. Can you give me any suggestions? Thanks!

3 participations

peruvianfab

Sept. 15 at 12:49 p.m.

How about something with grilled chicken? They often have a grilled chicken wrap or a chicken Caesar salad. Good luck!

Annasunny/iStock/Getty Images

walt2gfs

Sept. 16 at 10:03 a.m.

Relax and eat moderately! In an amusement park you burn a lot of calories; more calories than on a normal day. Maybe you can have some junk food then. But not a lot!

maryrord

Sept. 17 at 8:52 p.m.

Corn or popcorn. Or take some granola bar with you and drink a lot of water.

Tangente Design/ID/BR

Based on Hammill, Kristy; Bjelica, Alex. We Are What We Eat. *Holistic Thinking Kids*. 2017. Available at www.holisticthinking.org. Accessed on May 19, 2021.

15 Read the text and check the correct alternative.

What is the text about?

a. ☐ The best junk food in the world.

b. ☐ What to eat in an amusement park.

c. ☐ Good food at home.

16 Write **T** (true) or **F** (false).

a. **letninja** writes his question on September 14 at 2:31 p.m. [ ]

b. He is going to an amusement park today. [ ]

c. **letninja** wants to eat pizza, ice cream and French fries. [ ]

d. **peruvianfab** answers first and **maryrord** answers last. [ ]

17 Match the participants to their suggestions.

a. peruvianfab	( )	suggests corn, popcorn, granola bars and water.
b. walt2gfs	( )	suggests a salad or a wrap with chicken.
c. maryrord	( )	says that it's OK to eat some junk food on that day.

18 Write your suggestion to **letninja**.

- Decide on a nickname and draw an image of you if you want.
- Write the date and time.
- Think about good and healthy suggestions.
- Write your suggestions. They should be short and clear.

B I U abc
A A
Arial
12
Send

ID/BR

19 Discuss with your classmates and teacher.

a. What do you usually eat when you are not at home?

b. What healthy options can you find in amusement parks, in movie theaters, at the beach, etc.?

People who care

Conteúdo na versão digital

Values

Spend your money wisely

20 Plan one week of your vacation. You have $100 to spend.

Financial planning is very important for a successful vacation. Plan ahead of time! See how much money you have, the cost of the activities you want to do, and make smart choices by choosing your favorite activities and knowing your limits!

- collecting rocks or seashells – $0
- eating at a fast food restaurant – $10
- going to a museum – $10
- going to an amusement park – $70
- going to the movies – $20
- playing matkot – $0
- reading a book – $0
- swimming in the sea – $0

Mon	Tue

Wed	Thu

Fri	Sat

Sun

21 Discuss with your classmates and teacher.

a. Is it difficult to plan how much to spend on vacation?

b. Why is financial planning important?

Games and challenges

22 Find the hidden message. Follow the instructions.

- Work in groups of four.
- Read the text and find all the words related to food and drink. Some words are backwards.
- Delete those words.
- Read the secret message.

Tangente Design/ID/BR

ILOVECOLLECCHICKENTINGSEAREGRUB
SHELLSCHOCOLATEWHENI'MCOCONUTON
HSIFTHEBEACHSEIRF,BUTECIUJITIURF
DON'TICECREAMLIPOPCORNKEPLAY
SPAGHETTIINGMATDALASKOTRETAW.

Maria Pavlova/iStock/Getty Images

Shalamov/iStock/Getty Images

Workbook
Go to page **128**.

Let's read images!

Some languages around the world

1 Match the Stop signs to the right language.

Arabic Hebrew Hindi Korean Russian Thai

A

СТОП

Dmitry Evseev/Alamy/Fotoarena

B

ठहरिए

Dinodia Photos/Alamy/Fotoarena

C

หยุด

Chaiyapak Mankannan/Shutterstock.com/ID/BR

D

قف

Bruno Ismael Silva Alves/Shutterstock.com/ID/BR

E

정지

WorldStock/Shutterstock.com/ID/BR

F

עצור!

Arkadiy_Yarmolenko/iStock/Getty Images

2 Match the languages to the flags.

A

Imnature/iStock/Getty Images

Israel

B

Railway Fx/Shutterstock.com/ID/BR

South Korea

C

Nirian/iStock/Getty Images

Thailand

D

Anddraw/iStock/Getty Images

Russia

E

Black Pearl Footage/Shutterstock.com/ID/BR

Egypt

F

Menonsstocks/iStock/Getty Images

India

☐ 한국어 ☐ हिन्दी ☐ русский

☐ ไทย ☐ עִברִית ☐ عربي

Follow-up

1 Read and write **T** (true) of **F** (false).

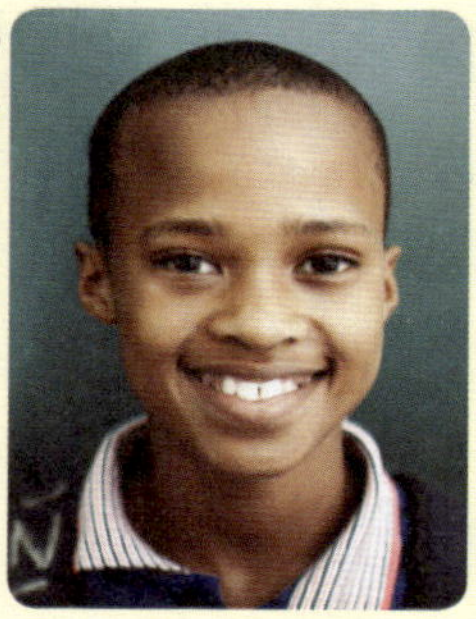
Steex/iStock/Getty Images

Hi, my name is Thomaz. I love playing musical instruments. I can play the drums, the keyboards and the guitar, but I can't play the piano or the bass. By the way, the guitar is my favorite musical instrument. It has six strings, it's not big and I can take it with me everywhere.

I love rock and pop music, but I don't like classical music very much.

a. Thomaz loves playing musical instruments.

b. He can play the drums, but he can't play the keyboards.

c. He can't play the piano.

d. He loves rock and classical music.

e. His favorite musical instrument is the drums.

2 Complete with **can** or **can't**.

Tobkatrina/Shutterstock.com/ID/BR

a. Danton ____________ play the piano because he has a bruise on his finger.

Borysevych.com/Shutterstock.com/ID/BR

b. Laura ____________ sing today because she has a sore throat.

VGstockstudio/Shutterstock.com/ID/BR

c. Tina ____________ play the drums very well. She is part of the school band.

Stock-Asso/Shutterstock.com/ID/BR

d. Paulo ____________ play the bass, but today he has a headache and he doesn't want to play.

How many ☺?

3 Look and write sentences about these kids.

How do they feel today?

Aslysun/Shutterstock.com/ID/BR

A

She ______________________________.

Vikram Raghuvanshi/iStock/Getty Images

B

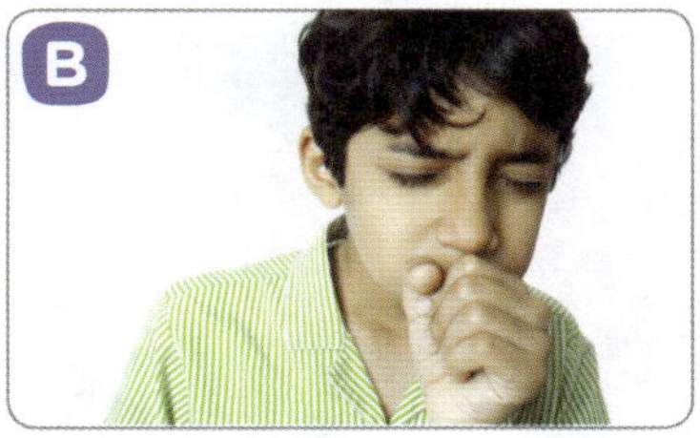

He ______________________________.

Shantell/iStock/Getty Images

C

______________________________.

Sabphoto/Shutterstock.com/ID/BR

D

______________________________.

4 Order the dialogue.

9nong/Shutterstock.com/ID/BR

- [ ] Tracy, you look tired! What's the matter?
- [ ] Why don't you drink some coconut water?
- [ ] What do you feel?
- [ ] What do you like drinking: juice or water?
- [ ] Well, I think I'll have a glass of water.
- [ ] Hmm, I don't like coconut water.
- [ ] I am a little bit dizzy and I have a stomachache.
- [ ] I feel sick today, Jackie.

How many ☺? [ ]

5 53 Listen and write the names.

Ricky Carlos Maria Amanda

Juanmonino/iStock/Getty Images

Emholk/iStock/Getty Images

Cameron Whitman/Shutterstock.com/ID/BR

Daniel Ernst/iStock/Getty Images

6 Read and circle the correct word.

Tangente Design/ID/BR
Elena Panah-Kritsimas/EyeEm/Getty Images

A: What do you like **do/doing** on vacation?

B: I love **going/go** to the beach.

A: What do you **doing/do** there?

B: I like **collecting/collect** seashells, but I don't like **swim/swimming**.

A: When I go to the beach, I usually **drink/drinking** lots of coconut water.

How many ?

7 Write the numbers.

a. 147: ____________________

b. 313: ____________________

c. 555: ____________________

d. 679: ____________________

e. 986: ____________________

How many ?

Karaoke
Go to page **112**.

GENERAL SELF-ASSESSMENT - UNITS 5-8

I know the name of some musical instruments and how to say if I can play them.	☐	☐	☐
I know the name of some health problems and how to say how I am feeling.	☐	☐	☐
I know how to say the color of the hair, eyes, and if someone is tall or short.	☐	☐	☐
I know the name of some activities people can do on vacation, some food items and the numbers up to 999.	☐	☐	☐

Karaoke

1 54 55 Write the words. Then listen and complete the lyrics.

Who'll Stop the __________

Long as I remember,
The __________ been comin' down
__________ of mystery pourin'
Confusion on the ground.
Good men through the ages
Tryin' to find the __________
And I wonder,
Still I wonder
Who'll stop the __________

I went down Virginia,
Seekin' shelter from the __________
Caught up in the fable,
I watched the tower grow
Five-year plans and new deals
Wrapped in golden chains
And I wonder,
Still I wonder
Who'll stop the __________

Heard the singers playin',
How we cheered for more.
The crowd had rushed together
Tryin' to keep warm.
Still the __________ kept pourin',
Fallin' on my ears
And I wonder,
Still I wonder
Who'll stop the __________

Lonely__/iStock/Getty Images

Sibgat/iStock/Getty Images

Auspicious/Shutterstock.com/ID/BR

Vik_Y/iStock/Getty Images

John Cameron Fogerty. *Who'll stop the rain*. Available at https://www.youtube.com/watch?v=lIPan-rEQJA. Accessed on April 26, 2021.

2 56 57 Listen, complete the lyrics and sing.

arms radio face dance heart
shoes eyes flower love

Let's ________

Let's ________ (x3)
Put on your red ________
and ________ the blues
Let's ________
To the song they're playin' on the
____
Let's sway
While color lights up your ________
Let's sway
Sway through the crowd to an
empty space
If you say run,
I'll run with you
If you say hide,
We'll hide
Because my ________ for you
Would break my ________ in two
If you should fall into my ________
And tremble like a ________

Let's ________ (x3)
For fear your grace should fall
Let's ________
For fear tonight is all
Let's sway
You could look into my ________
Let's sway
Under the moonlight, this serious
moonlight
If you say run,
I'll run with you
If you say hide,
We'll hide
Because my ________ for you
Would break my ________ in two
If you should fall into my ________
And tremble like a ________

Let's ________ (x3)
Put on your red ________
and ________ the blues
Let's ________
To the song they're playin' on
the ________
Let's sway
You could look into my ________
Let's sway
Under the moonlight, this serious
moonlight

Kipargeter/Vectorstock.com/ID/BR

David Bowie. *Let's Dance*. Available at https://genius.com/David-bowie-lets-dance-lyrics. Accessed on April 26, 2021.

Workbook

Unit 1 - Surfing the Web

1 Read the sentences and match them to the photos.

a. Ms Johnson chats with her friends on her tablet.

b. You have to click on this link to see the photos.

c. Bia listens to music online.

d. Matt loves to play games on the computer.

e. Joey reads a lot of e-mails on his tablet.

Quavondo/iStock/Getty Images

Petar Chernaev/iStock/Getty Images

Mjth/Shutterstock.com/ID/BR

Pixelfit/iStock/Getty Images

nicknames
Web
Imagens
Vídeos
Sobre
Nickname
A nickname is a substitute for the proper name of a familiar person, place, or thing, for affection or ridicule.
nickname - tradução português - dicionário inglês ...
Tradução de 'nickname' e muitas outras traduções em português no dicionário de inglês-português.
dicionario/ingles-portugues/nickname

Available at: https://duckduckgo.com/?q=nickname&t=hc&ia=web. Accessed on: May 16, 2021.

2 Read the text and complete.

Linda Yolanda/iStock/Getty Images

Hi, I'm Ian.

I really ________________ (like) to play online games, but I ________________ (use) the Internet for school a lot too. For example, I use it to search stuff for my homework. I always ________________ (check) the information on different websites, on books and with the teacher. You know, sometimes websites have incorrect information.

My dad ________________ (use) his laptop to work. He ________________ (read) and ________________ (send) e-mails every day, but he ________________ (not/surf) the Web a lot.

Cathy, my aunt, ________________ (live) with us. She ________________ (like) to chat with her friends on her phone, but she ________________ (not/send) many e-mails. She ________________ (read) a lot of books online too.

My sister Sam usually ________________ (watch) videos about Art on her tablet. She ________________ (study) Design at the university.

Well, my family and I ________________ (use) the Internet a lot at home, but we ________________ (play) board games and ________________ (go) to the park and to the club too. I really like to be offline sometimes!

Unit 2 - Pictures of the wildlife

1 Find the names of the animals and write them below the corresponding photos.

F	Y	A	R	M	A	D	I	L	L	O	U
D	S	E	A	T	U	R	T	L	E	I	O
H	U	M	M	I	N	G	B	I	R	D	J
I	E	O	S	D	E	V	B	Y	O	L	B
P	D	N	K	M	A	C	A	W	E	R	E
P	C	K	L	Q	S	H	A	R	K	W	A
O	T	E	U	S	R	A	O	A	S	G	R
A	I	Y	T	T	P	R	T	O	E	F	T

Heather Faye Bath/iStock/Getty Images

____

Angela Arenal/iStock/Getty Images

____

Burachet/iStock/Getty Images

____

Josef Fredhuber/iStock/Getty Images

____

Strmko/iStock/Getty Images

____

Picsbyaimee/iStock/Getty Images

____

RobinEriksson/iStock/Getty Images

____

Davemhuntphotography/Shutterstock.com/ID/BR

____

2 Complete the captions.

have   eats   stays   abandons   drinks   live

Edson Grandisoli/Pulsar Imagens

A A caiman sometimes ________________ all day in the same position.

RicAguiar/iStock/Getty Images

B A toucan often ________________ small fruits.

SerengetiLion/iStock/Getty Images

C In nature, the jaguar always ________________ water from rivers.

Edevansuk/iStock/Getty Images

D Golden lion tamarins ________________ an orange-yellow mane similar to a lion.

MaggyMeyer/iStock/Getty Images

E Lions ________________ in savannas, in Africa.

AlanJeffery/iStock/Getty Images

F The macaw never ________________ its mate.

Unit 3 - Going to the movies

1 Read and match the sentences to the photos.

a. My sister likes adventure movies a lot.

b. I like musicals and dramas.

c. My mom doesn't like sci-fi, but she likes animation.

d. I like animation, but I don't like action movies.

e. My cousins like comedy movies.

Walt Disney Studios Motion Pictures/Pixar Animation Studios/Everett Collection/Fotoarena

The Weinstein Company/Everett Collection/Fotoarena

Positive and negative icons: Tangente Design/ID/BR

Warner Bros. Ent. All rights reserved./Everett Collection/Fotoarena

KC Bailey/Disney +/Everett Collection/Fotoarena

Disney +/Everett Collection/Fotoarena

Walt Disney Pictures/Pixar Animation Studios/Everett Collection/Fotoarena

Universal/Everett Collection/Fotoarena

Universal Pictures/Everett Collection/Fotoarena

2 Read and complete the dialogues.

CINEART MOVIE THEATER

MOVIE	SESSIONS				
Lord of the Earrings	2:10 P.M.	4:35 P.M.	7:00 P.M.	9:25 P.M.	
Carrie Potter	10:50 A.M.	1:50 P.M.	6:10 PM	8:20 P.M.	
Pirates of the Bahamas	12:30 P.M.	2:20 P.M.	4:10 P.M.	6:00 P.M.	7:50 P.M.
Superdog 3D	11:05 A.M.	1:05 P.M.			

Tangente Design/ID/BR

a. **A**: Let's see ______________________. It starts at 8:20 p.m.

B: But I prefer *Pirates of the Bahamas*. The last session starts at ______________________.

b. **A**: I want to see ______________________, it's in 3D!

B: But there are only two sessions, and they are very early.

c. **A**: How about ______________________?

B: Great! We can see the 4:35 p.m. session.

d. **A**: *Carrie Potter*, here we go! Let me buy some popcorn.

B: We don't have time for popcorn. It's 1:45 p.m. and the movie starts at ______________________.

Unit 4 - Having fun

1 Look at the picture and answer the questions.

Sebastian
Julian
Tom
Anna
Sam
Mila
Patty
Carrie Potter

Raitan Ohi/ID/BR

a. Is Sam dancing?

____.

b. Is Patty reading comics?

____.

c. Is Tom chatting with Julian?

____.

d. Is Anna reading a book?

____.

e. What is Mila doing?

____.

f. What is Sebastian doing?

____.

2 Read and complete the dialogue.

hudiemm/iStock/Getty Images
Image Source/iStock/Getty Images

Sophia: Who are they, Arthur?

Arthur: They're my cousins. We're ______________ soccer on the beach.

Slawomir Fajer/Shutterstock.com/ID/BR
hudiemm/iStock/Getty Images

Sophia: What about this photo?

Arthur: This is my sister. She's ______________ to music in her bedroom.

hudiemm/iStock/Getty Images
AndreyPopov/iStock/Getty Images

Arthur: And this is my mom. She's ______________ e-mails and ______________ to my grandma on the phone.

Unit 5 - Sounds of music

1 Look and find the names of the musical instruments.

D P P F L D G U I T A R S G Y

H
G
Y
W
A
H
G
H
A
R
M
O
N
I
C
A

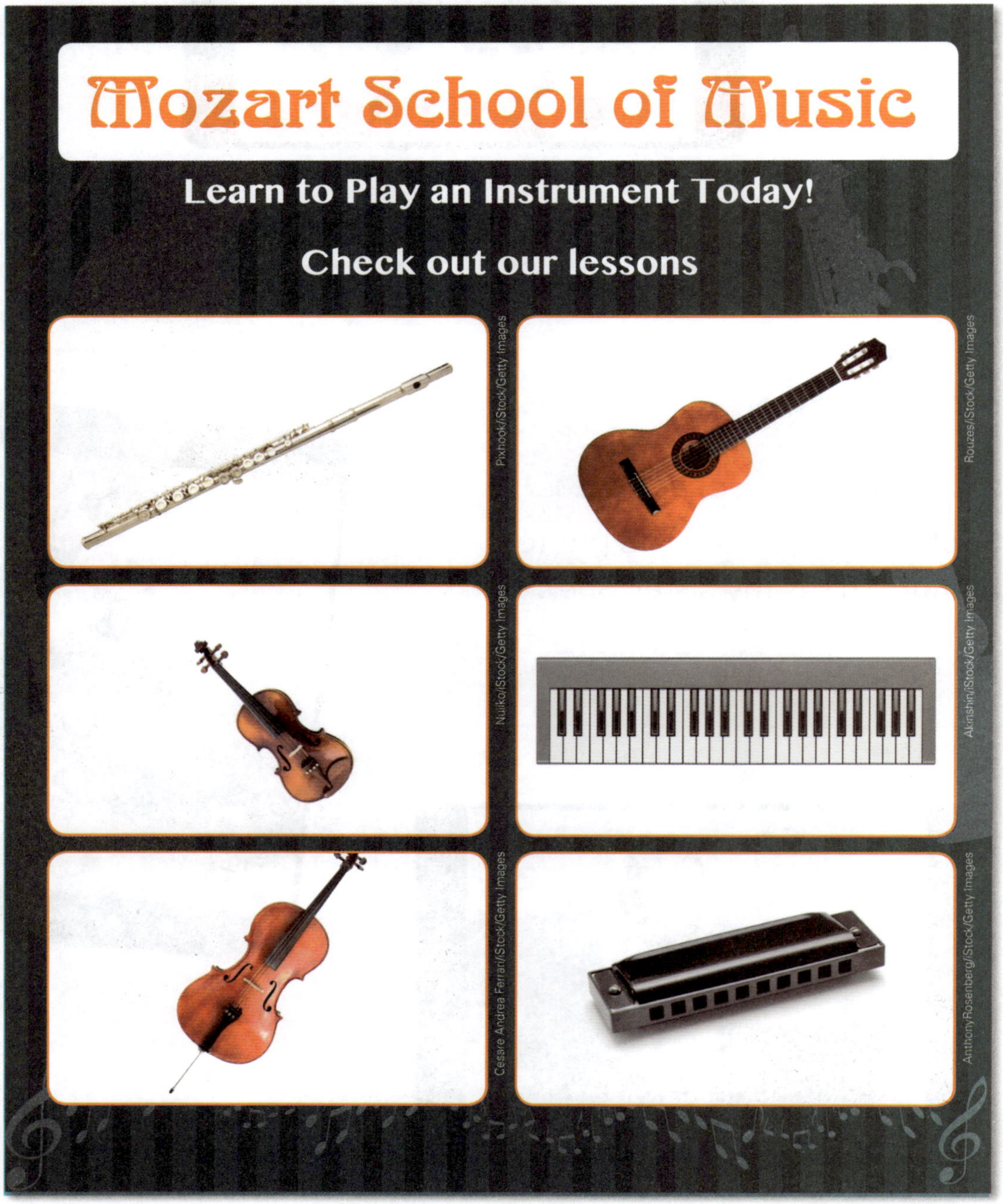

Mozart School of Music
Learn to Play an Instrument Today!
Check out our lessons
Pixhook/iStock/Getty Images
Rouzes/iStock/Getty Images
Nuiiko/iStock/Getty Images
Akinshin/iStock/Getty Images
Cesare Andrea Ferrari/iStock/Getty Images
AnthonyRosenberg/iStock/Getty Images
Mike Monahan/vShutterstock.com/ID/BR

H
K
E
Y
B
O
A
R
D
S
G
M
N
S
F
L
U
T

H P M N S V I O L I N K C E L L O E

2 Look and write sentences with **can** or **can't**.

a. He can play the flute ______________________.

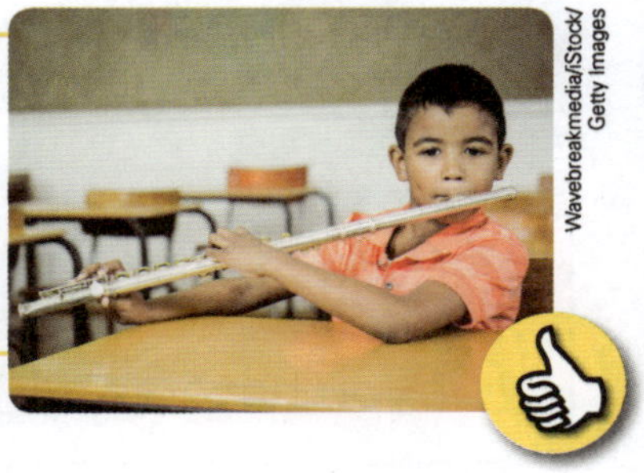
Wavebreakmedia/iStock/Getty Images

Bikeriderlondon/Shutterstock.com/ID/BR

b. ______________________

______________________.

Positive and negative icons: Tangente Design/ID/BR

c. ______________________

______________________.

Muzsy/Shutterstock.com/ID/BR

Skynesher/iStock/Getty Images

d. ______________________

______________________.

e. ______________________

______________________.

Christopher Futcher/iStock/Getty Images

Blaj Gabriel/Shutterstock.com/ID/BR

f. ______________________

______________________.

Unit 6 - I'm not feeling well

1 Look, read and complete the crossword.

Down ↓

1. If you have a ________________, you may have the flu.
2. If you have a ___________________, you may have food poisoning.

Across →

3. If you have a ________________, you may have tooth cavities.
4. If you have a ____________ nose, you may have a cold.
5. If you have a _____________, you may have pneumonia.

Baona/iStock/Getty Images
Makieni/iStock/Getty Images
Utah778/iStock/Getty Images
Skynesher/iStock/Getty Images
Sharon Barnes/iStock/Getty Images

2 Unscramble the words to complete the dialogues.

WHAT'S THE MATTER?

Jose Luis Pelaez/Getty Images

ProArtWork/iStock/Getty Images

A: I have a ____________________. (eehhcdaa)
B: Let's call the doctor.

Eric Audras/Onoky/Getty Images

A: I have an ____________________. (eeaahcr)
B: Let's go to an otolaryngology clinic then.

Paul Bradbury/Ojo Images/Getty Images

A: I have a ____________________. (sreo tthaor)
B: No ice cream for you then!

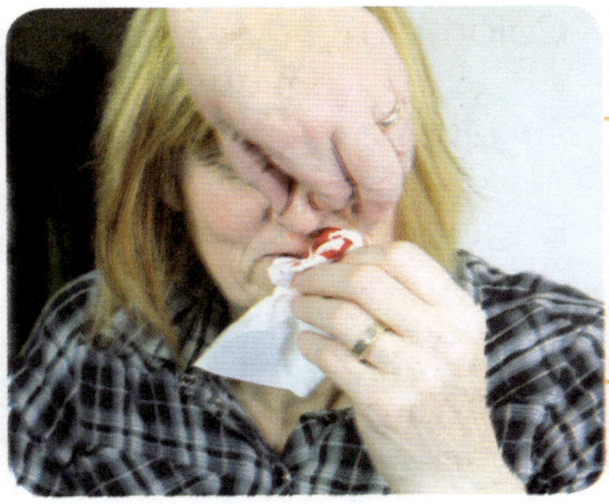

Henfaes/iStock/Getty Images

A: I have a ____________________. (ndoblseee)
B: Get out of the sun and lie down here.

Unit 7 - Expressing yourself

1 Read and match the countries to their corresponding language.

Do you know that some different countries speak the same language? For example, in Brazil we speak Portuguese, and in Portugal, Angola and East Timor they speak Portuguese too. English is another example. It is the first language of many countries, like the United States, Canada, England, Australia and South Africa. And many countries speak Spanish, especially in Latin America, for example: Argentina, Colombia, Mexico, Peru and Ecuador.

LANGUAGES

- **A** Portuguese
- **B** English
- **C** Spanish

COUNTRIES

- [ ] Brazil
- [ ] Australia
- [ ] Angola
- [ ] East Timor
- [ ] The USA
- [ ] Mexico
- [ ] Peru
- [ ] Portugal
- [ ] Canada
- [ ] South Africa
- [ ] Colombia
- [ ] Argentina
- [ ] England
- [ ] Ecuador

Christophe Testi/vshutterstock.com/ID/BR

2 Look, read and match the descriptions to each photo.

A

Gradyreese/iStock/Getty Images

I love spending my vacation with my uncle Barnie. He is very funny! He is tall, and he has short straight brown hair and a beard. We have a lot of fun together! ☐

B

Steele2123/iStock/Getty Images

My mom is very beautiful! She is tall, and she has curly brown hair and brown eyes. She is also my best friend! ☐

C

PeopleImages/iStock/Getty Images

My cousin Jonathan is ten years old and he lives in Canada. He is not very tall and he has straight red hair and blue eyes. He can speak English, French and Portuguese. ☐

D

Tsokur/iStock/Getty Images

Vivian is my granddaughter. She has long straight black hair and dark brown eyes. We love each other and we do everything together. ☐

E

Visionchina/iStock/Getty Images

I love visiting my grandpa José on vacation. He lives in another city, on a farm. He is very tall and he has straight white hair, blue eyes, and very big hands! We get fruit from the orchard together. ☐

Unit 8 - Vacation time

1 Unscramble the words and match them to the photos.

a. lrildeg hinkcce ______________________

b. nootccu artwe ______________________

c. amesdh ootapt ______________________

d. aesofdo ______________________

e. shfi lfilte ______________________

f. uftri asdla ______________________

Shaiith/iStock/Getty Images

Volosina/iStock/Getty Images

ClaudioVentrella/iStock/Getty Images

Tuned_In/iStock/Getty Images

Elena_Danileiko/iStock/Getty Images

Zhaojianhua/iStock/Getty Images

2 Complete the number puzzles. Then find and color.

Red: two hundred and twenty
Orange: seven hundred and seventy-two
Green: three hundred and eighty-eight
Blue: two hundred and thirty-one

↓ 10 more ↑ 10 less
→ 1 more ← 1 less

91		
		103
	112	

		211
219	220	

↓ 50 more ↑ 50 less
→ 1 more ← 1 less

670		
	721	
	771	

336	337	

3 Solve the cryptograms.

A	B	C	D	E	F	G	H	I	J	K	L	M
8	6			7	15		3	21	1		11	23

N	O	P	Q	R	S	T	U	V	W	X	Y	Z
	2	16	19	9	17	20	10		5	22	13	4

21	11 2 26 7	9 7 8 24 21 14 18	6 2 2 25 17.

21	11 21 25 7	12 2 11 11 7 12 20 21 14 18
	17 7 8 17 3 7 11 11 17.	

21	24 2 14 20	11 21 25 7	16 11 8 13 21 14 18
		23 8 20 25 2 20.	

21	3 8 20 7	17 5 21 23 23 21 14 18
21 14	20 3 7	17 7 8.

4 Create your cryptogram.

A	B	C	D	E	F	G	H	I	J	K	L	M

N	O	P	Q	R	S	T	U	V	W	X	Y	Z

Save endangered species campaign

Materials

Yuri_Arcurs/iStock/Getty Images

Art supplies

KittyVector/Shutterstock.com/ID/BR

Colored paper

GLUE STICK

17rst/iStock/Getty Images

Glue

Worldofstock/iStock/Getty Images

Colored markers

Steps

1. Choose a title for your campaign.

Save the Endangered Species
Help the animals

Illustrations: Werllen Holanda/ID/BR

Endangered Species

2. Research animal species that are endangered.

3. Create your poster, leaflet or both.

Save the animals

4. Present your work to the class.

Your silent movie

Materials

Props and costumes

Paper or poster board

Colored markers

GLUE STICK

Glue

Cell phone or tablet

Steps

1. Discuss the story (plot) with your teacher and classmates.

Illustrations: Werllen Holanda/ID/BR

2. Choose and prepare the scenery.

3. Write the title cards.

¡OH!
WHAT

4. Action! Shoot your video or take a series of photos.

Prevention booklet

Materials

Shmizla/Shutterstock.com/ID/BR

Paper

Yuri_Arcurs/iStock/Getty Images

Art supplies

ShutterOK/iStock/Getty Images

Scissors

GLUE STICK

17rst/iStock/Getty Images

Glue

Diana Taliun/iStock/Getty Images

Yarn

Steps

1. Research tips to prevent an illness, for example, dengue.

Pre
ven
tion
Dengue
PREVENTION
Dengue
Fever

Illustrations: André Santos/ID/BR

2. Decide what information, drawings, and photos you want to put in your booklet.

3. Create pages for your booklet.

Glue

Be Healthy
PREVENTION IS THE
BEST REMEDY

4. Put these pages together and make the booklet.

Artwork

Materials

Subjug/iStock/Getty Images

Recyclable material

Yuri_Arcurs/iStock/Getty Images

Art supplies

KittyVector/Shutterstock.com/ID/BR

Colored paper

Shmizla/Shutterstock.com/ID/BR

Paper or poster board

Zinkevych/iStock/Getty Images

Modeling clay

Steps

1. Talk about artwork with your teacher and classmates.

Tarsila do Amaral
Abaporu

Illustrations: André Santos/ID/BR

Tarsila
TARSILA
Tarsila

2. Choose an artist and research about his/her life and artwork.

3. Choose an artwork and create your version of it.

INK

4. Exhibit your artwork to the class.

Classroom Language

Teacher

Ask your neighbor for help.
Peça ajuda ao vizinho.

HappyKids/iStock/Getty Images

Don't forget to bring your ____ next class.
Não esqueça de trazer seu/sua ____ na próxima aula.

Do you have any questions?
Vocês têm alguma pergunta?

We'll continue this unit next class.
Continuaremos esta unidade na próxima aula.

This is your homework for next class.
Esta é a tarefa de casa para a próxima aula.

Why were you absent last class?
Por que você faltou à aula passada?

You have five minutes to do this.
Vocês têm cinco minutos para fazer isso.

Juice Flair/Shutterstock.com/ID/BR

Student

Can I join your group?
Posso entrar no grupo de vocês?

Can you help me do this exercise?
Você pode me ajudar a fazer este exercício?

Can you speak more slowly, please?
Pode falar mais devagar, por favor?

How do you say ____ in English?
Como se diz ____ em inglês?

How do you spell ____?
Como se soletra ____?

_it
_ip
_in
_ill
dip hip lip rip sip tip zip trip flip ship
bill fill gill hill Jill mill pill will drill chill

FatCamera/iStock/Getty Images

I have a question.
Eu tenho uma pergunta.

ElenaMist/iStock/Getty Images

What does ____ mean in Portuguese?
O que ____ significa em português?

When is the homework for?
Para quando é a tarefa de casa?

Instructions and commands

Complete the crossword to find the missing words.

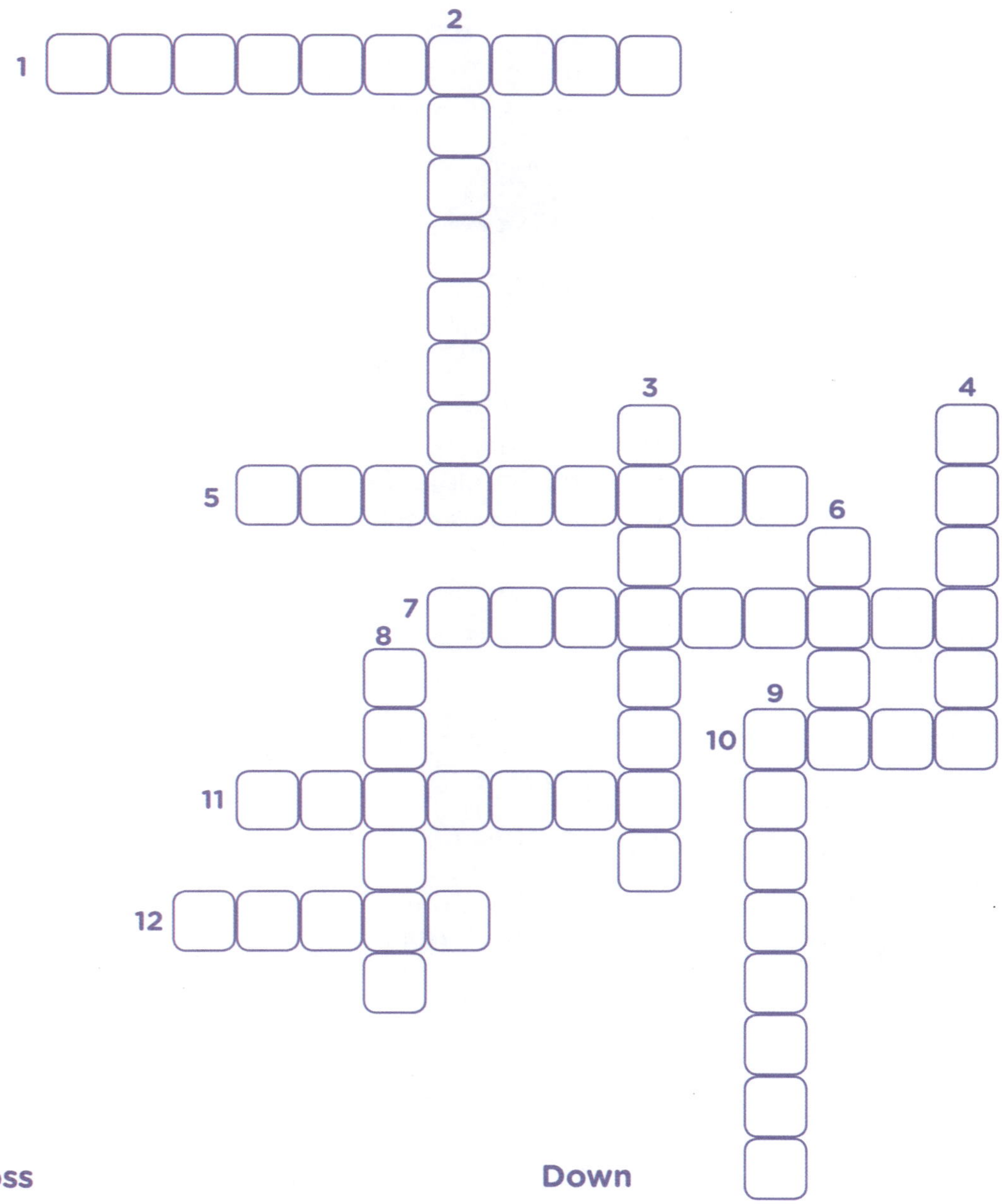
1
2
3
4
5
6
7
8
9
10
11
12

Across

1. ______________ the words.

5. ______________ the wrong answer.

7. ______________ the right word.

10. See you ________ Tuesday!

11. ______________ the sentences.

12. How do you ______ your name?

Down

2. Correct the ______________.

3. Don't forget your ______________.

4. She is __________ today.

6. __________ your favorite animal.

8. Speak __________, please!

9. Help your __________.

Glossary

Welcome - Summer camp

about: a respeito de, sobre
among: entre (várias coisas, pessoas, etc.)
armchair: poltrona
behind: atrás
beside: ao lado
between: entre (duas coisas, pessoas, etc.)
cleaner: faxineiro(a)
climb: escalar
eat: comer
eighty: oitenta
feed: alimentar
fifty: cinquenta
forty: quarenta
in: em (dentro de)
in front of: na frente de
lamp: luminária, abajur

Marynka Mandarinka/Shutterstock.com/ID/BR

live: viver, morar
living room: sala de estar
ninety: noventa
nurse: enfermeiro(a)
on: sobre, em cima de
pick up: colher, apanhar
rabbit: coelho
ride: andar de bicicleta; andar a cavalo
season: estação
seventy: setenta
sixty: sessenta
skate: andar de *skate*
ski: esquiar
something: algo, alguma coisa
summer camp: acampamento de verão
thirty: trinta
toy: brinquedo
twenty: vinte
under: embaixo de
wake up: acordar

Unit 1 - Surfing the Web

agree: concordar
because: porque (motivo)
bookworm: pessoa que gosta muito de ler

Serhiy Kobyakov/Shutterstock.com/ID/BR

bullying: ato de intimidar e humilhar alguém
buy: comprar
careful: cuidadoso(a)
channel: canal
chat with: conversar com
click: clicar
date of birth: data de nascimento
dinner: jantar
ditch: eliminar
download: baixar (da Internet)
file: arquivo
find: encontrar, descobrir
hungry: faminto(a)
insulting: insultante
laptop: computador portátil
later: mais tarde
maybe: talvez
mind (don't mind): importar-se (não se importar)
need: precisar
nickname: apelido
password: senha
permission: permissão
personal: pessoal
print: imprimir
ready: pronto
receive: receber
recipe: receita
search: buscar, procurar
search engine: ferramenta de busca
send: enviar
share: compartilhar; dividir
should: dever
social media: mídia social
software: programa de computador
surf the Web: navegar na Internet
trip: tropeçar
understand: entender
walk: caminhar
watch: assistir a

Unit 2 - Pictures of the wildlife

always: sempre
amazing: espantoso
armadillo: tatu
bear: urso
beautiful: bonito(a)
caiman: jacaré
capybara: capivara
carapace: carapaça, casco
change: mudar

colorful: colorido
dangerous: perigoso
disappear: desaparecer
dolphin: golfinho

Tory Kallman/Shutterstock.com/ID/BR

dried plant: planta seca
endangered: ameaçado de extinção
environment: meio ambiente
everyone: todos(as)
extinction: extinção
fast: rápido
female: fêmea
frog: rã
fur: pelo
governor: governante
ground: solo; chão
heavy: pesado
hippo: hipopótamo
hole: buraco
hummingbird: beija-flor
interesting: interessante
jaguar: onça-pintada
lay (egg): botar (ovo)
lion: leão
macaw: arara
male: macho
mammal: mamífero
mane: juba
mate: companheiro(a)
meat: carne
monkey: macaco
nest: ninho
never: nunca
often: frequentemente
polar bear: urso-polar
population: população
recycle: reciclar
reduce: reduzir
reduction: redução
reptile: réptil
reuse: reutilizar
shark: tubarão
skin: pele
sloth: bicho-preguiça

Jonathan Ross/iStock/Getty Images

slow: lento
snake: cobra
sometimes: às vezes
species: espécie(s)
spot: mancha
tail: cauda
toucan: tucano
trade: mudar
tree: árvore
turtle: tartaruga
tidy: limpo; organizado
vegetable: vegetal
web of life: teia da vida
whale: baleia
wildlife: vida selvagem

Unit 3 - Going to the movies

3D glasses: óculos 3D
action: ação
actor: ator
actress: atriz
adventure: aventura
after that: depois disso
a.m.: antes do meio-dia
animation: animação
as well: também
buy: comprar
cast: elenco
cell phone: celular
character: personagem
check: verificar
choose: escolher
comedy: comédia
danger: perigo
decide: decidir
devotion: devoção
enjoy: aproveitar, curtir
fantasy: fantasia
fifties: anos 50
first: primeiro
juice: suco
kick: chutar
last: último
less: menos
line: fila
loud: alto
movie: filme
movie theater: cinema

ODEON
FANATICAL ABOUT FILM
Bikeworldtravel/Shutterstock.com/ID/BR

planet: planeta
p.m.: depois do meio-dia
popcorn: pipoca
sci-fi: ficção científica
session: sessão
silent movie: filme mudo
soda: refrigerante
synopsis: sinopse, resumo do filme

Glossary

then: então, depois
through: através
ticket: ingresso, entrada
trash: lixo
trash can: lata de lixo
turn off: desligar
vacation: férias
villain: vilão; vilã
wear: usar, vestir

Unit 4 - Having fun

afternoon: tarde
alone: sozinho
be in trouble: estar encrencado
bowling: boliche
breakfast: café da manhã
chat: conversar, bater papo
comic strip: tirinha
comics: gibi, história em quadrinhos
countryside: campo, área rural
create: criar
dance: dançar

Christopher Futcher/iStock/Getty Images

dinner: jantar
drawing: desenho
evening: início da noite
free time activities: atividades de lazer
fool someone: enganar alguém
gang: turma
go to bed: ir dormir, ir para a cama
ham: presunto
hang out with friends: passar tempo com amigos
have a good time: divertir-se
have lunch: almoçar
hold on: aguardar, esperar
jump rope: pular corda
meet: encontrar
morning: manhã
Muslim: muçulmano
near: perto, próximo
night: noite, madrugada
prayer: oração
rescue: resgate
same: mesmo
say a prayer: fazer uma prece, rezar
selfie: foto de si próprio
skill: habilidade
soccer: futebol
stage: estágio
swim: nadar
there: lá; aí
uncle: tio
volleyball: vôlei

Unit 5 - Sounds of music

amazing: fantástico
arrive: chegar
bass: contrabaixo
beat: batida
belief: crença
can: ser capaz de
castanets: castanholas
cello: violoncelo
concert: concerto, *show*

Goran Djukanovic/Shutterstock.com/ID/BR

diversity: diversidade
drums: bateria
electric guitar: guitarra elétrica
flute: flauta transversal
guitar: violão
half note: mínima (meia nota)
harmonica: gaita
keyboards: teclado
own: próprio
perform: apresentar-se (em espetáculo ou *show*)

play: tocar
proud: orgulho; orgulhoso
quarter note: semínima (1/4 de nota)
rehearsal: ensaio
saxophone: saxofone
seem: parecer
singing class: aula de canto
slave: escravo
style: estilo
tambourine: pandeiro

Djmilic/Shutterstock.com/ID/BR

triangle: triângulo
violin: violino
whole note: semibreve (nota inteira)

Unit 6 - I'm not feeling well

allergy: alergia
arm: braço
bite: picada; mordida
bruise: machucado, contusão
buddy: amigo, camarada
cavity: cárie
cold: resfriado
contagious: contagioso
cough: tosse; tossir
cover: cobrir
defense: defesa
dizzy: tontura
earache: dor de ouvido
everybody: todos(as)
feel: sentir
fever: febre
fight off: combater
flu: gripe
food poisoning: intoxicação alimentar
get rest: descansar
hand: mão
headache: dor de cabeça
juicer: centrífuga, equipamento de preparar sucos

Ivan Bajic/iStock/Getty Images

matter: problema
mix: misturar
mouth sore: feridas de boca
nauseous: enjoado, com náusea
nosebleed: sangramento no nariz
nothing: nada
nurse: enfermeiro(a)
prescription: prescrição, receita médica
prevent: prevenir
recipe: receita
red spot: mancha vermelha
rest: descanso
runny nose: coriza
serve: servir
shake: agitar
side: lado
sneeze: espirrar
sneezing: espirro
sore throat: dor de garganta
spoon: colher
spread: espalhar
stagnant water: água parada
stomachache: dor de estômago
tablet: comprimido
take care: cuidar
throw up: vomitar
tip: dica
toothache: dor de dente
vitamin: vitamina
wash: lavar
win: ganhar

Unit 7 - Expressing yourself

beard: barba
beautiful: bonito
blaze: inflamar, flamejar
blond: loiro
body language: linguagem corporal
Brazilian: brasileiro, brasileira
bright: brilhante
brown hair/eyes: cabelos/ olhos castanhos
canvas: tela

TeerawatWiny/iStock/Getty Images

curly hair: cabelos encaracolados
darkness: escuridão
detail: detalhe
France: França
French: francês, francesa
German: alemão, alemã
Germany: Alemanha
gesture: gesto

Glossary

gray hair: cabelos grisalhos
haze: névoa
Italian: italiano, italiana
Italy: Itália
Japanese: japonês, japonesa
look like: parecer
long hair: cabelos longos
Mandarin: mandarim
painter: pintor
painting: pintura
panel: painel
Portuguese: português, portuguesa
portrait: retrato

Tetiana Lazunova/iStock/Getty Images

realistic: realista
red hair: cabelos ruivos
sad: triste
sculpture: escultura
self-portrait: autorretrato
short: baixo (em estatura)
short hair: cabelos curtos
soul: alma
South Africa: África do Sul
Spanish: espanhol, espanhola
starry: estrelado
straight hair: cabelos lisos
swirling: rodopiante
tall: alto
tourist guide: guia turístico
wood: madeira

Unit 8 - Vacation time

amusement park: parque de diversões

Elesi/Shutterstock.com/ID/BR

arts and crafts: artesanato
backward: de trás para a frente
calorie: caloria
chicken wrap: enrolado de frango
choice: escolha
coconut water: água de coco
collect: pegar; coletar
collection: coleção
cook: cozinhar
cost: custar; custo
eight hundred: oitocentos
everything: tudo
expensive: caro
far away: distante, longe
fish fillet: filé de peixe
five hundred: quinhentos
four hundred: quatrocentos
French fries: batatas fritas
granola bar: barra de cereais
grilled chicken: frango grelhado
healthy: saudável
ice cream cone: casquinha de sorvete
junk food: comida não saudável

Valentyn Volkov/iStock/Getty Images

mashed potatoes: purê de batatas
matkot: frescobol
nine hundred: novecentos
one hundred: cem
sea: mar
seafood: frutos do mar
seashell: concha
seven hundred: setecentos
shrimp: camarão
six hundred: seiscentos
smart: inteligente
soft drink: refrigerante
spaghetti: espaguete
string: corda
swimming pool: piscina

Press outs

Pages 15, 47, 77 • Dice, pawns and cards

Tangente Design/ID/BR

Instruction

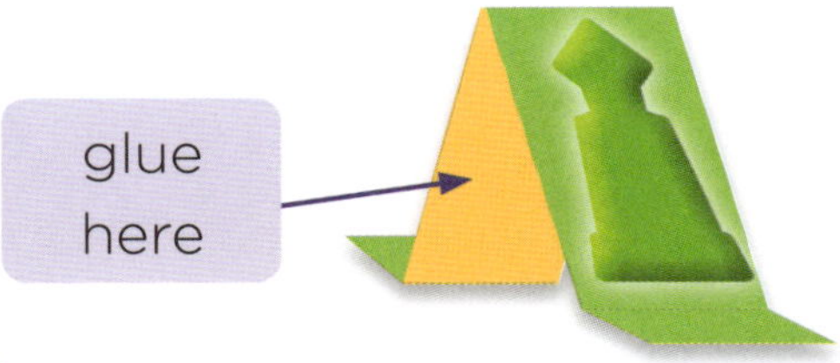
glue here

Mime you singing.	Draw a guitar.
Mime you playing the violin.	Draw a flute.
Mime you have a headache.	Mime you playing the drums.
Draw a person with a toothache.	Mime you are dizzy.
Draw a person with a runny nose.	Mime you have a sorethroat.

Press outs

Page 30 • Cards

AllanPin/iStock/Getty Images
MR1805/iStock/Getty Images
Whitepointer/iStock/Getty Images

Cinoby/iStock/Getty Images
Ken Canning/iStock/Getty Images
JasonOndreic/iStock/Getty Images

Martin Mecnarowski/Shutterstock.com/ID/BR
Fabio Colombini/Photographer's collection
Ondrej Prosicky/Shutterstock.com/ID/BR

It's a reptile.
It lays eggs.
It can swim
and walk.

It's white and big.
It lives in cold places.
It can swim.

It doesn't have legs.
It can be long or short.
It changes its skin.

It's a Brazilian bird.
It's colorful and it's
endangered.

It's a big mammal.
It lives in the oceans.
It can swim.

It's a big fish.
It can attack humans.
It's dangerous.

It's a bird.
It can visit more than
one thousand flowers
a day.

It's small.
It can make holes on
the ground or can roll
into a ball.

It's a reptile.
It lives near the water
and eats meat.

Press outs

Pages 121, 123 • Cards

THE SMURFS 3
JULY 2015
TheSmurfs-Movie.net
3:15 p.m.

Columbia Pictures/Sony Pictures Animation/ID/BR

MARY POPPINS
11:45 a.m.

Walt Disney Pictures/ID/BR

MODERN TIMES
CHARLES CHAPLIN
10:05 a.m.

Charlie Chaplin Film Corporation/ID/BR

SHREK
3:05 p.m.

DreamWorks Animation/ID/BR

THE PEANUTS MOVIE
IN THEATERS
NOV 6
7:05 p.m.

Twentieth Century Fox Animation/ID/BR

THE LION KING
4:35 p.m.

Walt Disney Pictures/Buena Vista Pictures/ID/BR

Phichet Chaiyabin/Shutterstock.com/ID/BR

Julia Kuznetsova/Shutterstock.com/ID/BR

Isitsharp/iStock/Getty Images

Tyler Olson/Shutterstock.com/ID/BR

Photolyric/iStock/Getty Images

Diane Diederich/iStock/Getty Images

Christopher/iStock/Getty Images

Ti-ja/iStock/Getty Images

SinceLF/iStock/Getty Images

Orange Line Media/Shutterstock.com/ID/BR

Press outs

Pages 90, 98 • Cards

Mangostock/Shutterstock.com/ID/BR

Jorg Hackemann/Shutterstock.com/ID/BR

Gadelshina Dina/Shutterstock.com/ID/BR

Warrengoldswain/iStock/Getty Images

Nataliia Romashova/Shutterstock.com/ID/BR

ChompooSuppa/Shutterstock.com/ID/BR

$10

MarKord/Shutterstock.com/ID/BR

$20

D13/Shutterstock.com/ID/BR

$50

Marco Rubino/Shutterstock.com/ID/BR

$15

Iuliia Timofeeva/Shutterstock.com/ID/BR

$5

Helen Sushitskaya/Shutterstock.com/ID/BR

$25

Karisssa/iStock/Getty Images

$420

Billion Photos/Shutterstock.com/ID/BR

$18

Barcin/iStock/Getty Images

$1

Janifest/iStock/Getty Images

$3

Kwangmoozaa/iStock/Getty Images

Stickers

Page 13 • Look and stick.

Welcome

BETWEEN	ON	IN FRONT OF	BEHIND
BESIDE	IN	UNDER	AMONG

Page 23 • Read and stick. Then complete the sentences.

Unit 1

Nickname Generator

Available at: https://www.namegeneratorfun.com/nickname. Accessed on 28 May, 2021.

DuckDuckGo
nicknames kids
New to DuckDuckGo? Take a Tour

Available at: https://duckduckgo.com. Accessed on 17 May, 2021.

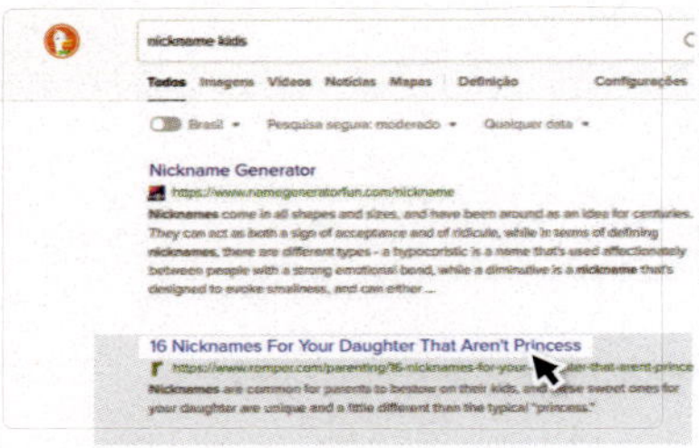
nickname kids
Nickname Generator
16 Nicknames For Your Daughter That Aren't Princess

Available at: https://duckduckgo.com/?q=nickname+kids&t=hd&va=u&ia=web. Accessed on 28 May, 2021.

Page 24 • Read the text and stick.

Unit 1

Online Friends	Social Networking
Bullying and Insulting	Your Name on the Net
Passwords	Photos
Personal Information	Downloading

Stickers

Page 32 • Read and stick.

Unit 2

Scanrail/iStock/Getty Images

Simone van den Berg/Shutterstock.com/ID/BR

Super Prin/Shutterstock.com/ID/BR

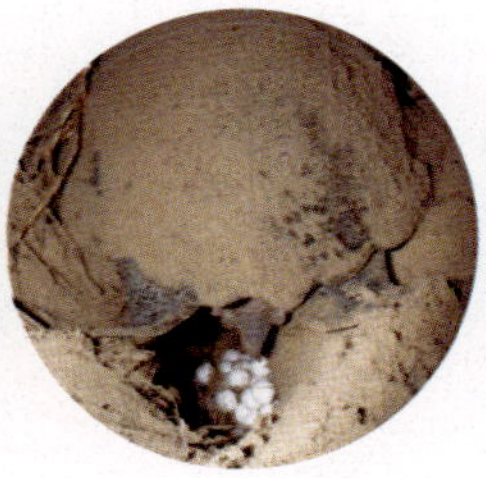
Danikancil/iStock/Getty Images

Page 46 • Read, stick and then circle or cross out.

Unit 3

Karramba Production/Shutterstock.com/ID/BR

Bonnie Schupp/iStock/Getty Images

Colin Hawkins/Getty Images

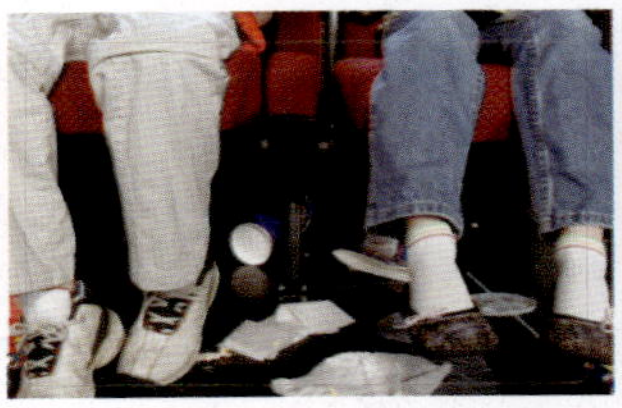
Fuse/Corbis/Getty Images

Altrendo Images/Shutterstock.com/ID/BR

Page 50 • Look and stick. Then check the items you like.

Unit 4

movies	bowling
rope	music
friends	drawings
photos	comics

Stickers

Page 72 • Read, unscramble and stick the correct photo.

Unit 5

Asier Romero/Shutterstock.com/ID/BR

DenisFilm/Shutterstock.com/ID/BR

Diogoppr/Shutterstock.com/ID/BR

Page 82 • Read the text and stick.

Unit 6

Mauricio Simonetti/Pulsar Imagens

Huronphoto/Getty Images

Ramona Heim/Shutterstock.com/ID/BR

Warat42/iStock/Getty Images

Stickers

Page 92 • Read and complete the infoboxes. Then stick.

Unit 7

Louvre Museum, Paris. Photography: ID/BR

Museum Casa Guignard, Ouro Preto/Raquel, Isabel e Helena Lacerda. Photography: Heitor Cavalheiro

Page 101 • Listen, circle and say. Then stick.

Unit 8

4kodiak/iStock/Getty Images

Vm/iStock/Getty Images

Tirc83/iStock/Getty Images

Melissandra/iStock/Getty Images

Tassapon/iStock/Getty Images

Gargolas/iStock/Getty Images